Praise for *Re-enchanting the Fc*

In today's Western world, we are richer than
of technologies, foodstuffs and consumer goods available to most of us
would have rendered our ancestors speechless. We are told almost daily
how lucky we are. So what is this huge hole at the centre of our culture?
What is this grief that lurks beneath the surface? What is this thing we are
missing, that so many of us can sense, but few can put their finger on?

It is, I think, a lack of understanding of our place in time and history, our
loss of a deeper place in the natural order of things, a dim sense of our
broken connections with the world beyond the human. A rediscovery of
ritual is part of the necessary work to bind up this wound, and this book is
a powerful part of the remedy.
Paul Kingsnorth, activist and author of *The Wake* **and** *Real England*

By introducing people to the ways of ritual, William Ayot helps people
towards a wiser, richer, more connected life.
Sobonfu Somé, initiated teacher, activist and author of
The Spirit of Intimacy

This is the most compelling book I know on the vital but lost role of
ritual in our lives. Neither an academic treatise nor a theological tract,
Re-enchanting the Forest is about life as it is and might be lived in a secular
world, a book that honoured my mind but reached directly into my heart
and soul. I cannot recommend it highly enough, with only one caveat:
reading it might change your life as it changed mine.
Parker J. Palmer, author of *A Hidden Wholeness* **and**
Healing the Heart of Democracy

In this remarkable book, William Ayot reclaims the beauty of practical
ritual to enhance our lives, to heal, to inspire and to reveal personal
insights otherwise beyond our ken. Ritual comes home. We can welcome
it back and hold it close to our hearts.
Professor Brian Bates, author of *The Way of Wyrd*

William Ayot guides us masterfully through the theory of ritual and its cultural heritage into its very essence.
Nicholas Janni, founder of Core Presence
Associate Fellow, University of Oxford Said Business School

I love the way William Ayot's book combines the story of his life with an exploration of the value and purpose of ritual. By weaving the accounts of his own challenges, described with such heartfelt honesty, with discussions of how to work with ritual, the whole subject comes alive. I found I couldn't stop reading.
Philip Carr-Gomm, author of *Druidcraft* and *Sacred Places*

Besides being beautifully written, gripping and moving, this book is important. At a time when humanity is slowly shifting from driven logos to connection and nurture, we need tools to bring us back into the stream of our personal and collective lives. William Ayot, in amazing, unpretentious simplicity, offers us ways to remember the rituals and ceremonies that have guided humanity since the dawn of time. In the United States, where I live, the split between detached and connected is particularly deep. The ideas and stories presented here are sure to have an impact on those consciously ushering in a different age.
Laurence Hillman, astrologer and author of *Planets in Play*

William Ayot takes the mysterious and elucidates it with simplicity, practicality and clarity while lifting the apparently ordinary to the realm of mystery. If you have shied away from religion or ceremony yet instinctively know there is a more-than-human world to engage in somewhere, this beautiful book is for you.
Richard Olivier, artistic director of Olivier Mythodrama and author of *Shadow of the Stone Heart*

William Ayot introduces us to the art and application of ritual in one of the most clear, insightful and illuminating accounts I have ever read. Many books claim that they will change your life - this one doesn't - but if you let it, this book can work away at you from the inside, providing guidance and encouragement until you find your own courage, seek out your own rituals, and re-enchant your own life.
Andy Logan, co-founder of the Praxis Centre,
Cranfield University School of Management

Through the kinds of authentic ritual that William Ayot shares with us in this wise and generous book, we can all learn to experience a different kind of knowing: one that cares deeply for our souls.
Geoff Mead, author of *Coming Home to Story* and
Telling the Story: The Heart and Soul of Successful Leadership

Beautifully written and profoundly important for our times. This book speaks to an ancient and urgent need directly and accessibly - it's a very potent work.
Nick Ross, Director, A Different Drum

Perhaps our age is both the most abstracted and the most materialistic ever. We need to find new ways of expressing our current confusion and our longing for re-connection. Ritual – like art – builds bridges into the dream-time where some of the answers lie. William Ayot's book has roots in a wiser past, and branches that stretch into a more embodied future.
Professor David Peters, Clinical Director,
Westminster Centre for Resilience,
Faculty of Science and Technology, University of Westminster

One of the most important and inspiring books I have ever read in the field of ritual practice. William Ayot shows us that ritual is nothing to be scared of. It is instead a vital aspect of an integrating psyche, as relevant and essential today as ever, and a true ally to well-being, perspective and purpose.
Ben Walden, Founding Director, Contender Charlie

This is a powerful book, a handy source to rediscover the lost art of rituals.
Satish Kumar, Editor-in-Chief of *Resurgence & Ecologist Magazine*

About the Author

William Ayot was born in rural Hertfordshire. Having worked in London's casino industry, he underwent a personal transformation, rejoining the world as a poet, teacher and ritualist. He has worked in rehab, prisons, and men's groups, led rites of passage and taught in boardrooms and business schools around the world. William is a member of the Welsh Academy, and an FRSA. He lives in a restored Monmouthshire gentry-house with his wife, psychotherapist Juliet Grayson.

Also by William Ayot:

Theatre
Bengal Lancer
Shakespeare's Ear

Poetry
The Water-Cage
Small Things that Matter
The Inheritance
E-Mail from the Soul:
New & Selected Leadership Poems

Choral Music
Anyone Can Sing
(composer Andrea Ramsey)

www.williamayot.com

Re-enchanting the Forest

Meaningful Ritual in a Secular World

William Ayot

First published in 2015 by Vala Publishing Co-operative

Sleeping Mountain Press edition published in 2016

Copyright © William Ayot

Sleeping Mountain Press
Courtyard House, Moynes Court,
Mathern, Chepstow
Monmouthshire, NP16 6HZ

Front cover illustration by Ron Pyatt

Cover design by Rachel Dickens

ISBN 978-0-9930306-5-9

Preface

We have a rich, sophisticated culture in the West, but we live in a world of ritual poverty. We have neither healing rituals for parents who have lost a child, nor rites of passage to initiate our troubled youth. We have nothing to instil the elderly with a sense of value and purpose, and nothing whatsoever to greet the returning warrior, changed beyond help and hurt beyond all kindness. Most bizarrely of all, we have nothing to mark or cauterise the end of a twenty-year relationship that began in a flurry of white lace and ended in petty cruelties and recriminations.

And yet there is a part of us that yearns for living ritual; an ancient, deeply attentive part that knows the stars and the weather, and the names of the trees. It doesn't do email but it has stories in its heart and songs that it took from the birds, and it is sure of itself, very sure of itself, out there in the forest. *Re-enchanting the Forest* was written for that part of us.

The book charts the journey of my life in ritual, as a seeker, a student and latterly as a practitioner. It was conceived as a way of showing that there are rituals that can serve secular people today, rituals that are neither superstitious mumbo-jumbo on the one hand, nor empty New Age pap on the other. I also wanted to show that the supposedly 'primitive' ritual cultures of Africa, Asia and the Americas are no such thing – that in fact they have a great deal to show us, and that the indigenous way of ritual has its own, very sophisticated technologies.

Spending time with tribal medicine teachers, it soon became apparent to me that we in the West needed to rediscover our own ritual tradition. This had been sundered by an industrial revolution, the Enlightenment, and over a century of mechanised warfare. We needed the medicine teachers' help because only they could take us into the ritual spaces with which we had lost contact. Once there, they could show us the techniques and practices that we could then tie together in a brand new, but authentically re-woven, tradition of our own.

Unfortunately we in the West have a history of raiding and destroying indigenous cultures. Medicine teachers are rightly wary of passing on their rites and methods to us, however keen we might be to learn. Our past crimes can often arise in their viscerally lived histories. Occasionally, in private conversation with a tribal elder, usually at the point where I asked an informed or technically competent question, I have felt a sudden chill. At times like these I could see dark questions forming behind an elder's eyes. "Let me get this right: you've taken our land, you've taken our resources, and you've taken our dignity ... now you want us to hand over our rituals?"

Yet I was lucky. I turned up at a point when my teachers were exiled from their native lands, or tasked with seeking an audience for their tribal wisdom. Without exception they were willing, generous and courageous dispensers of their endangered, sacred technologies. Even so, these often delicate relationships with our teachers were never purely transactional. No one was selling off their tribal secrets or buying Manhattan for a song. There was a tacit understanding that we had come together in troubled times. We knew that our teachers' cultures were under extreme pressure, and that they were urgently passing on their knowledge in the hope that we might revive our own uprooted traditions. Neither was it about copy-cat ritualising. As the archetypal psychologist and teacher Robert Moore once mentioned to me in conversation: "These guys did not come here for you to copy their religions. They're here to blow on the embers so you guys can get your own fires started again."

Over the years I have tried to make a start, sorting through the seeds of what I learned from my teachers, and replanting what was appropriate in the deep loam of my own culture. Occasionally, until such time as a home-sourced equivalent became apparent to me, I've kept to a tribal methodology or form to 'keep the flame alive'. I still use certain West African (Dagara, Tiv or Yoruba) chants, for example, because the rhythms of Africa are familiar to us through soul music and the blues, and we have no similarly evocative chants of our own. Gradually, as with the use of oats and mead, I have settled on specifically European practices to pass on to those who come after me. My hope is that they will modify what they receive from me, and begin the long slow process that is the ritual regeneration of our common, indigenous soul.

I am neither a priest nor a therapist – nor would I wish to be – but as a ritualist I acknowledge a duty of care and confidentiality around those I have served. In writing this book I have therefore felt free to name and reflect on my teachers whose work is in the public domain, while protecting the identities of those who have come to me for rituals. I have sought and received permission to share all the stories in the book, but I have changed names and places, wherever possible, for the rituals that I have led.

One of the more odd effects of ritual is that one's perception of time and events can become distorted. I have occasionally reflected this in the book's structure, as I've stepped out of the strict 'unities' of time and chronological sequence. If this is confusing to those who have shared numerable experiences with me, I can only apologise in the name of clarity and a readable narrative. Any other errors are mine and mine alone.

This book then is an attempt to provide some engaging information about meaningful ritual, for those who live in today's largely secular world. In writing, it became clear to me that it might also serve those who already employ ritual in their lives, and that it might even be of interest to those who facilitate and lead ceremonies in a clerical context. Whatever your place on this spectrum, I sincerely hope this book serves you.

William Ayot
Monmouthshire
June 2015

Foreword by Mark Rylance

William Ayot is an explorer. This marvellous book is a testament of his expeditions into the unknown. It is a testament to his ability to discern a path in wilderness, his ability to find water to drink where it's dry, and most vitally his willingness just to survive in unknown places. It is also a testament of the extraordinary landscape, the sacred time, the subtle wheel of fortune, we can find ourselves in when we awaken, as William does, before the dawn. William is also a poet.

Did you ever get up in the muddle before dawn
for no better reason than that you wanted
to greet the sunrise?
Did you ever dress quietly, with serious intent,
and pick your way over wintry fields
to arrive at a place that you once imagined
bathed in the first clear light of morning?
And did you wait as the dawning grey,
moved through purple, to mauve, to grey,
from excitement to boredom, to a kind of calm
as you gently noticed your insignificance?
And did you mutter unfamiliar words
that seemed to come from somewhere else,
ancient words of dread and devotion,
words of welcome and astonishment?
And when at last the tired sun
issued from the earth like a molten copper head,
did you notice the hawk that flew at you,
rose in a way that made everything sacred,
stooped in a way that made the day blaze?

Or did you sleepwalk into the morning,
bending your dreams to another's purpose,
listening to the news, half hoping for a cataclysm,
anything to make the tired day more real.
(A Challenge; Email from the Soul)

William calls his poem "A Challenge". I take it as a challenge to be awake in the muddle before our own minds dawn. Ritual for me has been a way of wakening. I experienced rituals with some of the same teachers William did and have employed them in my work since. I have maintained, for nearly twenty-five years, a ritual with friends to mark the eight solar and lunar festivals of the year. I have found pilgrimage deeply satisfying and I celebrate significant anniversaries and find certain landscapes sacred. I suspect you, reader, will have many rituals yourself, rituals of health and cleanliness and holiday, family rituals. William leads us into a deeper appreciation of ritual and reading this book I feel in the presence of an authentic leader. Here is a guide who has criss-crossed the terrain he speaks of. Here is a man who has slept out in it, who has listened late and heard the song that many dismiss as the random, unmusical noise of existence. Here is a humble man who has learnt through mistakes. A man of thoughtfulness.

I love "the tired sun" in this poem. It reminds me of the important role of tiredness in ritual. Deep tiredness. Being tired is a kind of gateway. It reminds me of a physical trainer who tires out one set of abdominal muscles in order to get another set, lazy beneath, to lift your torso from the ground. Reminds me of spare tyres and new tyres. The flaming tyres of Phoebus' Cart, rolling over the horizon. To explore ritual is to enter the world of inter-being, inter-meaning, that poets best enjoy.

Across the great plains beneath the commercial cross-country jet in which I am reading and writing this foreword today, I see the square grid of modern American agricultural life. I see its rationale broken only by the old rivers and the new highways that trail beside them. I see in the past a group of Lakota people evading the dangers East and progressing slowly West. I see Black Elk as a boy being ritually healed and his visions enriching his people. Do we not also progress, as a people, across great plains pursued now by our own culture of domination and separation from Nature. This is the industrial landscape of our time. Ritual is like an old meandering river in the grid. It just connects it to the landscape I am observing from the plane. I am flying west to meet my brother in a ritual we have sustained for over ten years. Every year or so, we walk and sleep in the mountains for four or five days. This ritual began when we remembered how our favourite times as boys were the adventures we had together. As adults we were beginning to only meet at Christmas and other formal family occasions. We created a ritual to sustain our brotherhood love for wildness and for each other. Always, when we set out into the high sierra, we give gifts and sing a song of thanks to the nature we are about to walk through.

But William is writing here about ritual in a more profound manner. William includes Pilgrimage in this introduction to the potent role of ritual in life. Ceremony too. He recalls his own pilgrimage towards a ritual place, from childhood to his present day, with such detailed memory and natural re-discovery that I feel I am indeed walking with him. As in a well-acted play, I am frightened with him. Lonely with him. Relieved, excited, curious and astonished beside him. One of our favourite teachers told us of an indigenous people who believed that the universe was created and sustained by a song. An archetypal song. A harmony of the universe. The beautiful song of their gods. They believe that when we sing or create anything beautiful in ritual, when we put our souls into it, we contribute to and help to sustain that creative song of the gods that in turn sustains all creation; a song singing a song singing a song singing a song... I understand all matter to be vibrating energy, which is also sound, so the song of creation is not so far-fetched as it may at first appear. This non-personal, non-psychological ritual work, with no benefit to the participant other than the benefit of creation and appreciation, this perhaps is the deepest ritual work, the most profound.

I met William in a time, a passage of my life, full of ritual, ceremony, and what? Curiosity. The men around me in 1996-97 seemed more curious than they perhaps had been, other than older men I knew. My curiosity was restless, active, imaginative, dark, and just beginning to look back into my past life at more apparent waves left behind me, or patterns around me. As if I had been a rock dropped in a pond. Often the patterns revealed, in my case, behaviour that seemed ready for a change. I wanted to change, to grow. I longed like the muscles of my legs longed when I was a teenager. How they ached in the night and my mother would say it was their growth pains.

In my experience, we gathered, the curious ones, most powerfully and consciously under the straightforward penetrating gaze of the great mid-western farmer's son, Robert Bly. Held by his imagination and gripped by his eloquent ability to lead a large group of men, drawing us out of ourselves with humour, wonder and honest affection, praise, he would pour us back into ourselves within the dark forest of an old tale from the Brothers Grimm.

I remember someone once calling it the men's "expressive" movement and indeed, Robert could express so beautifully the place where we were, the time, during the different experiences of a four day retreat, selecting words from his wide and hungry love of poetry. By the time I got involved Bly had become practised at finding the resonant note, the key change through a poem, amongst a group of men. He spoke much sufi poetry, sacred poetry from many lands and languages. He was not alone: James Hillman, Michael Meade, Malidoma Somé, and sadly one who wishes not to be named in this book ... these were our Elders. We always concluded with a profound ritual, often a celebration of the feminine.

And there was William, the gatekeeper, holding the door open. Just how many doors he had opened in his own mansion, I have only begun to grasp reading this very personal book. He was always at the heart of it.

> It is the lack we notice.
> The crowded years of coffee-rush ---
> of back-to-back meetings and poker faces,
> of sucking up and drilling down,
> of saying yes when you really mean no ---
> all lead to a night in a nondescript room
> above some anonymous, rain-soaked town.
> You find yourself looking down at the traffic
> crawling its way through the sodium glow.
> You catch your reflection. You hear yourself
> speaking: I am not the person I wanted to be.
> (Acorns and Angels; Email From The Soul)

Like William, in the nineties, I had become fascinated by the Eleusinian mysteries of the ancient Greeks. The idea of a mystery school of experience, a school through experience, an experience, emotional, physical, spiritual, that fed the soul's hunger. Could this be a theatre experience? Our mutual friend, Richard Olivier, had a similar hope and it was Richard's enterprising and imaginative spirit that both William and I chose to partner, I in the theatre opening The Globe and William in an organisation called Wild Dance that brought to England Robert Bly and all his good fellows, from archetypal psychologists to initiatory shaman. Suspicious eventually perhaps of our workshop culture, Wild Dance transformed into mythodrama work and William, Richard and a small group of friends moved into the hard world of business and brought ritual bravely into the private and public work place.

The poem above captures that bleak landscape before the dawn. But it also speaks universally, I feel. Here is an experience I have felt, though I have never been a travelling salesman.

What did we learn? It's hard to sum up. We learned the role of beauty and integrity in one's communication with the spiritual realm of existence. We learned the necessity of the soul's role in carrying messages between perceived and imagined polarities, bridging them. We awakened to the appetite of our own soul and witnessed that Soul is unbounded by rules and divisions of the mind. Suddenly our soul was speaking through the landscape, trees, animals, weather, coincidence of time. The wit of the soul! The irreverence and wildness. The love of disguise and ambiguity. But the occurrence that struck me most was when we grieved. Ninety men vocally grieving together, dropping our tears onto a black stone placed in our midst and then singing a song of hope for the young men who had rejoined our meeting when they heard us making an undeniably authentic sound. This was a ritual I will never forget. This was a blessing.

I wonder if both Manners and Ritual have a bad name today. When you think of manners do you think of suburban Sunday dinners with no elbows on the table, middle class Lady Bracknells holding forth, while Oscar Wilde sits in Reading jail? I grew up with an impression that manners were a cover, an avoidance of intimacy, politeness rather than truth. I longed to be with the rude folk because they said what they felt. Do you feel the same way about Ritual? Are rituals something that take place in school, in boardrooms, outside Buckingham Palace and inside the houses of Parliament, on Christmas Day? Are they just meaningless routines to keep the ruling power in power? I think it was James Hillman who once praised the role of good manners and changed my mind. James spoke of manners, good manners, ideally creating the space for emotional discussion, shared engagement, hard truth, intimacy. William Ayot revives here the potent and ancient role of ritual as anything but a meaningless routine to keep the powerful in power. Quite the contrary.

I hope you feel inspired by his tale, as I do.

Mark Rylance
August 2015

- To the Grandfathers -

and
to the memory of

Dr Chris Seeley

Contents

Chapter One

A Journey of a Thousand Miles

Forget explanations. Just do ritual. All will become clear.
Malidoma Patrice Somé

I was in my late thirties when I finally stumbled into the world of
ritual. Close to burnout, I had been working in the gaming industry
for twenty years, since losing my childhood home in Hertfordshire
and drifting down to London. Mildly dyslexic, and still a teenager, I had
applied for a job as a courier and ended up as a croupier in one of London's
newly legalised casinos.

"Why d'you wanna work for us?" asked the manager.

"Well, I've always wanted to travel," I said, innocently enough.

"Okay, smart-ass. Show me your hands."

I put out my hands, which showed him that I didn't bite my nails – you
can't deal Blackjack if you bite your nails – and, too embarrassed to explain
my mistake, I stuck around, and learned to deal cards. Then I got paid – an
astonishing amount of money for an eighteen year old – and found myself
working in Soho, which in those days was still London's red-light district;
a fascinating world of low-lifes, and arab princes, gamblers and gangsters,
pimps and hookers. Like other young drifters, I settled into this world and
promised myself that I would move on soon enough. I didn't. It was safe
and anonymous and it allowed me to quietly opt out of my life.

Thus, like a half-grown salmon, swimming out into the Atlantic,
I entered the long years of my gaming career, moving from Soho on to
Chelsea, and then up to Mayfair and Knightsbridge. After more than twenty
years of aimlessness and drift, I knew that my life was bleeding away. I'd
been writing plays in my free time with the occasional little success, and
one transfer to London, but even that had brought me little joy. By my late

thirties I was lost and depressed, emotionally numb and spiritually empty.

One quiet summer's evening, while I was working a double shift in the casino, I fell into conversation with a sprightly old lady who used to haunt the Blackjack pit where we'd both washed up. I had a soft spot for her and felt that her Jewish humour and direct way of speaking were familiar to me. This particular evening she was talking about where her family came from. I suddenly realised who she reminded me of – it was Ivy Isaacs.

Ivy Isaacs was a local hairdresser when I was a lad, a hard-headed, successful Jewish businesswoman in the nearest town who had taken me under her wing, having seen something worth nurturing in the lonely, dysfunctional teenager that I had become. For my part, I was fascinated by Ivy; everyone seemed to admire her strength and acumen but they were wary of her too. Her directness scared people. I was mesmerised by her wicked sense of humour and her deliciously shocking use of language. I used to hang around at the end of the day, sweeping up in her salon, waiting for her next gloriously foulmouthed outburst while she 'titivated' herself by adjusting her teeteringly baroque hair-dos, and what she called her war paint: a make-up so weirdly and wildly applied that it made me think of the clowns at Bertram Mills Circus, or Dusty Springfield in a tribal mask.

I hadn't thought of Ivy for years and I was ashamed. How could I have forgotten this extraordinary woman: her laughter, her fierceness, her dogged sense of survival, her kindness and her generosity? How could I possibly have blocked her out of my life?

Walking home from the casino, through St James's Park and over Westminster Bridge, I worried at her memory, pulling at it, fleshing out odd incidents as they arose. By the time I had curved my way round the deserted South Bank and on to Borough, I had put together a mosaic of forgotten fragments, snippets of language and memories. It was as if a door had creaked and swung open.

As I approached the square where I lived, other faces began swimming up out of my past: faces from my teens and schooldays, images from my time at boarding school, a hundred occurrences and dozens of long-forgotten faces. And then, as from the bottom of a well, I became aware of a circle of elderly faces from my childhood village: old men and women, mainly maiden ladies as they were called back then – a group at first, then individual faces – each one smiling sadly, silently asking to be remembered. At home, I sat for what felt like hours as they visited me, these sweet gentle old people, and I slowly began to realise why I had shut them out of my life. I couldn't bear the pain.

22

Most of the time, I was the only child in the village I lived in. As I grew up, I was surrounded by a tragedy common to hundreds of villages across Europe. Nearly all the men of my village had been killed during the First World War. Wiped out, almost to a man, on the Western Front. They had left behind a shattered circle of women: widows and fiancés, mothers, sweethearts and sisters, most of whom were in their sixties by the time that I turned up – a solitary, golden-haired boy who loved to listen to their stories. I absorbed their infinite sadness as they filled me with tea and biscuits, and treated me like Sunny Jim, a miraculous little demi-god, upon whom they could shower all the love and affection they had been unable to find a home for. I seemed to be the perfect audience.

It started to rain outside, and I remembered a miserable, wet, winter afternoon with Ivy Isaacs. I had popped in to see her but, by her own estimation, she was poor company. The plate-glass window of her salon was steamed up and dripping, shutting out the town and giving the place a closed-in, steamy, oppressive feeling. Ivy perched on her plastic-covered barstool behind the reception desk, her hair still plain and as yet unadorned. Sensing her mood, I leant on the reception desk and watched her intently as she stared at the condensation, which ran down her weeping window. I waited.

"They're all gone," she said at last, very quietly. "Mama, Papa, Zayde and Bubbe … aunts, uncles, cousins … all gone. Only my brother survived. He left me here and went on to Israel, but he was killed in '48. He's buried in Jerusalem. He's the only one of us that has a grave. One day, I'll go to Jerusalem, and when I do, I'll place a stone for him. I'll place a stone for every one of them. Every single one."

Ivy turned and looked at me as I shifted uncomfortably, staring down at the huge diamond rings on her claw-like fingers. She lifted my head and placed a tender hand on my cheek. "We have to remember – or we are nothing."

~

I remembered those stones as I walked up through the woods towards the Hertfordshire village where I spent my childhood. At thirty eight, I had no real understanding of what I was doing, but looking back, I can see that I was instinctively reaching for ritual as a way of dealing with something – something that was haunting me – long after it should have been laid to rest. There was something I had to do that day.

By the spring, where the brook gushes out, I clambered down into a steep-sided gully, where I straddled the bed of the once familiar stream. I started to look for treasure, as I used to as a boy. A careful climb down the gully soon brought me to a fallen tree trunk and beneath it a sandy bank. I ran my hands through the wet silt, relishing the chill of the water, and dredged up what I had been looking for – a handful of polished pebbles, glistening wet, their colours and shadows clear and bright. I rinsed them off and made my selection: little planets of orange-veined marble, darker blues that may once have been flints, and gobs of chert with their iron-stained and roughened peel. I sat back on the bank and listened to the silence.

I climbed out of the gully, cupping the pebbles, like a boy holding birds' eggs against my belly, I reached the path again, turned left and headed uphill. As I walked along, I took the pebbles one by one: rolling them between my fingers, polishing them against my trouser leg as their rich colours faded and they dried to a common dullness. I walked on, head down and pensive, close to an emotion that I was not yet able to name. For weeks I had been nursing an indeterminate feeling, a pain somewhere between guilt and shame (I hadn't yet learned how to distinguish the two) and something much deeper than my habitual gloom – a nameless, shapeless, bottomless ache.

The Welsh have a word, which has no equivalent in English. *Hiraeth* speaks of a yearning, a deep nostalgia for place. Not so much a homesickness, as something deeper, layered with grief, rooted in the loss of those we have loved; composted and enriched with deposits of sadness; a deep and abiding melancholy, fed by a particular soil and its ancient, ever-present dead.

This was the feeling that had brought me back, though I'd yet to find a name for it, still less acknowledge it as truly mine. Like a blind and tired salmon, I was sliding up the pebbled stream of my belonging, seeking out the one shaded pool that birthed me, the village that grew me, the place that I'd carried, hidden in my heart, ever since I was exiled as a lad.

~

So here I am with my pockets full of drying pebbles, walking towards the village that I left twenty-odd years before. Coming out of the woods, I feel the sun hot on my face as I cross the service road and walk over the bridge that leads to the village green. Below me six lanes of tarmac carry hundreds of cars between London and the North. Their roar fills the canyon gouged out of the hill. Midway across the bridge I feel a momentary vertigo, but

I am soon past it and walking onto the village green for the first time in years. The sudden quiet envelops me and I pause. It is as if nothing has changed.

To my left, a long wall is flanked by a number of horse chestnut trees. Their dense shade and carpet of brown leaves used to be the territory of a tribe of fierce little bantams. Ruled by a fearless Old English Game cockerel, who would face down any curious pet dog who strayed over onto his turf. But they are all gone.

The place seems real enough but some essential core seems to be missing. The trees – stag-headed oaks for the most part – are still there but everything seems that much tidier. The pond is less of a watering trough for passing cattle and more of a 'feature' within a landscaped garden, with water-lilies from a garden centre and reeds planted for effect. The grass verges are clipped and manicured, the cottages and houses immaculately maintained, extended or restored, with new windows and conservatories. I feel a hard unmanageable lump within me that I've occasionally felt but never acknowledged before. It feels like it could choke me.

I am a stranger here now. I walk on unnoticed and unwelcomed, moving through the village like a ghost; past the old farm and the gamekeeper's cottage, past the sawmill which smells of freshly sawn cedar, and on, uphill again between high hedges, towards the village church. Finally, I turn into the churchyard. I know why I am here now. I know what the stones are for.

That said, I don't know how to proceed. The lump inside me has grown and grown. I'm finding it hard to manage the intensity of feeling that walking through the village has stirred up in me. I sit down on the grass verge by the war memorial.

I know that they must be here but I don't know exactly where. My mother has told me of odd deaths over the years, and sent me the occasional notice cut out of a local paper, but I've never added them all together. I am suddenly, shockingly aware that nearly all of my childhood friends are going to be in this graveyard. It's one thing to pick pocketfuls of pebbles at a distance with a vague idea in your head, but quite another to confront your losses and make an act of remembrance by placing stones on a dozen or more graves. As I sit, a robin trills from a nearby gravestone. The liquid beauty of his song grabs my attention and somehow galvanises me. I make a decision and let the robin be my guide. He flits away as I approach and I see that he is perched on Peter Mardley's headstone.

Peter Mardley was the only other kid in the village, though he was slightly older than me. We played together before he went off to boarding school and I envied him his huge and elaborate train set which his father had put together, up in the roof of their home, Brock's Cottage. I can see Brock's Cottage now, over the fields, as I stand by Peter's grave. I remember my sudden anger on hearing that he had come home one day, and hanged himself, in the barn where we used to swing for hours on an old length of rope that was always hanging from a beam. Today, anger long-spent, I kneel by his headstone and place a first stone in remembrance.

I stand and cross the churchyard, seeking the cooling shade of the yew trees. Behind the church, I look down and see the grave of Jabez Dudley. Jabez was in his late eighties by the time I left the village. A real old Hertfordshire Hedgehog, as Hertfordshire men used to call themselves, he had been a gamekeeper and sniper during the First World War and one of the very few surviving men who came back whole. He taught me to shoot on an old double-barrelled .410, which had been given to him by the late King George the Sixth, whom he had also taught to shoot when *he* was a lad. Jabez had taken me out hunting woodpigeon for the pot, filling me with terrifying tales of snipers in no man's land, sharing his deep understanding of the woods and the seasons. His respectful way of paying attention, and his soft, slow Hertfordshire way of speaking had stayed with me over the years. He used the old Hertfordshire dialect address of 'old'n', as in "old boy". I choose a perfectly spherical piece of chert – like an old lead shot – and place it on top of his headstone, hearing his voice as I turn away, "Now there's a kindness, old'n ..."

And so my unplanned ritual unfolds, from grave to grave, sometimes following the robin, sometimes just wandering down the rows of graves. Farmer Warboys, and the Misses Farr; Miss Greatorex with her cage of chattering finches; Mrs Savage and Mrs Saul with their Hertfordshire stories and lardy cake; and tiny Gwen Hossack whose annual trip to the grave of Anna Pavlova, the great ballerina, sweetened her for a fortnight, every year.

And then I find Lawrie, quite by chance, tucked into the grave of a brother or a cousin – "Also Ellen Lawrence" – almost an afterthought. Lawrie, with her tidy grey bun and her sensible shoes, her lilac-sprig frock and her scent of lavender. Lawrie whom I fled to, whose simple ritual was the endless offering of love. Lawrie who had gently kissed me when I went away to boarding school, but whose cottage was boarded up when I came home. Lawrie whom I loved, and who had somehow slipped away.

At the churchyard gate I look back and see a dozen or more pebbles dotted among the headstones – each one reminding me of the meetings and the quiet village rituals I had witnessed as a child: from beating for the shoot, and storing apples, to chill November mornings with the whole village gathered by the war memorial.

Ivy! With a jolt I remember Ivy Isaacs, and her family. She must be long dead by now. I imagine her buried in Golders Green, where she lived, or maybe, just maybe in Jerusalem. I feel in my pockets, where there are still a few small pebbles left, and I cross to the war memorial. One by one I place a row of individual stones – one for Ivy, one for her brother, one for her parents, one for her grandparents, and another – quietly, delicately – for her unknown relatives lost in the horror of the Shoah. Their namelessness really bothers me.

I have one pebble left, a piece of grey-blue stone, ground and polished to oval perfection. I pop it in my mouth, wetting it with saliva so that when I take it out it glistens like a tiny blue planet. Slowly, I place it on the top step of the memorial. For Ivy and her dead; for the dead behind the names; for forgotten people everywhere; and for my own troubled dead, who are buried elsewhere. "We have to remember – or we are nothing."

~

This impromptu visit to my old village reconnected me to myself, through ritual, in profound ways, but there were no tears. Like many men I was still too shut down to actually weep, though I re-discovered a natural solemnity that spoke of a deeper grief that was still waiting to happen. As it evolved then, this was not a grief ritual – I hadn't yet discovered that there was such a thing – nor a cathartic purging of feelings. It was about reconnection, about owning my unacknowledged debt to these forgotten people; of speaking their names quietly in the afternoon stillness and making my peace with the ground that held them.

In doing the ritual, my soul, or psyche if you prefer, had come to accept that, despite the loss of the people, I still somehow belonged here. It was about reaffirming my identity, not staking a claim; it was about who I was and where I came from. I had run away from myself, trying to avoid my history, and in doing so had become an empty suit. In London, I had lived a series of roles – croupier, writer, helper, friend – but they all felt false. They were false. By going back to my village and ritualising the process of return, by smelling its sawdust and seeing its battered landscape, I had stepped onto my own turf again. I had come home.

By the time I got back into the woods, I was tingling with a sense of aliveness. My perception seemed to have changed by doing the ritual. I was lighter if not happier. I was taking more in. I began to assimilate some of these new experiences. Did a robin actually speak to me? I doubted it, but the experience in the moment was enough to lead me from grave to grave, and take me to the heart of the matter. Also – and this was real enough to stay with me – the robin's attention had made me feel less alone in a place of extreme loneliness. I began to remember other robins perched on spades, accompanying my elderly friends as they worked in their gardens. I began to see, in a simple village way, how connected we humans are with the world of nature, and how disconnected I had become.

Chapter Two

Sometimes Just to be Here is a Victory

This is what rituals are for ... to create a safe resting place
for our most complicated feelings of joy or trauma,
so that we don't have to haul those feelings around with us forever.
Elizabeth Gilbert, *Eat, Pray, Love*

In a better world, my parents would never have married. They were
thrown together at the de Havilland aircraft factory during the Second
World War. She was painfully thin, having overcome tuberculosis,
while he was an orphan and a divorcé, a sensitive man who never discovered
his art. He was also an alcoholic.

After the war they took a pub, and it was all downhill from there. The
first winter he broke his back in a drunken car crash and became a semi-
invalid. She then lost a baby who survived eight days and died of a hole in
the heart. Such was the wisdom of the day that she was told to get over it
by having another baby. I was therefore born to a mother who had yet to
grieve the loss of her firstborn and to a father who was drowning in grief.
To make matters worse, I was born without a roof to my mouth, without
a soft palate, which meant that when my mother fed me, the milk ran out
through my nose. I was lucky in that I was taken to Great Ormond Street
Hospital for Sick Children, where I was given a series of operations by
a surgeon who was an expert in the new and rapidly evolving discipline
of plastic surgery. This involved grafts, which built up a soft palate. The
downside was that my parents were told by the plastic surgeon that I would
never speak properly and that I would never, ever, sing.

As with most operations there was a degree of 'collateral damage':
invisible side effects that only became apparent later. In my case my hands
were tied to my cot to prevent me putting them in my mouth. The result

of this was that I had inexplicable nightmares until my mid-forties, waking exhausted, with my arms above my head. The other, more lethal effect of the operation was that my mother, who had been kept away from the hospital by work, was, through no fault of her own, unable to pick me up and hold me when I needed to bond with her. As her underlying sense of shame and failure kicked in, she was unable to express the love that she may well have felt for me. It was to take me forty-five years of often desperate chasing to learn that I was never going to get the love that I needed from my mother.

What happened was that my father filled the gap. Having buried my sister before me and seen me operated upon, he was determined that I would confound the surgeon's prediction and, one day, speak the Queen's English impeccably. Baby-talk was banished from the home and, despite having a kind of dyslexia, I was taught to read long before I started school. By the age of four, I would stand at the end of my father's sick-bed reading aloud to him as he lay there in the metal corset he had to wear. He coached me, teaching me to repeat the stories he was always making up for me. On slow afternoon walks around our village, he encouraged me to name things out loud – not just a tree, but an oak tree, or an elm, a sycamore or a rhododendron. The cows in the local fields were given names, as were the pigs, and the chickens. By the age of nine I was speaking with a cut-glass accent and singing my heart out at every opportunity.

One winter's evening, when I was about ten years old, I sang the opening solo at my prep school's carol concert: "Once in Royal David's City". As I stood in the transept of the ancient country church where the service was being held, I was nervous and excited, and acutely aware that I was a vital cog in some vast ceremonial mechanism. As I sang, I saw my father reaching out and holding my mother's hand, something I'd hardly ever seen them do before. I also became acutely, embarrassingly aware of my father crying, as tears streamed down his face.

In many ways my father was a remarkable man. He was just unlucky. He'd once studied for the priesthood and had been a student of mysticism back in the 1930s. His mother had died giving birth to him and he went to a string of boarding schools that left him ever more damaged. By the time I came along, he was a deeply hurt and needy man in his forties, desperate for some kind of love, and already in thrall to the alcohol that was to kill him.

As the darkness gathered and my mother was shut out, the scene was set for something approaching a tragedy. Slowly, inexorably, the alcohol overwhelmed us all. Boundaries were blurred and, at first, under the guise of medical examinations and procedures, lines were crossed that should never have been crossed.

I've heard it said that anything less than nurture is abuse. In that case I was clearly an abused and neglected child. My father didn't set out to hurt me, but the cruel truth is that I was a victim of what came to be called the Chosen Child Syndrome. As the sole focus for my father's love, I became a kind of surrogate spouse, providing the intimacy and attention that he had yearned for from the cradle, and the wholehearted adoration that my mother was unable to provide. In a way the sexual aspect was secondary – it was love he craved – but as time passed and the drink clouded everything, the line was crossed and the harm was done. From the vantage point of fifty-odd years, the physical hurt was less damaging than the invasion of my will and spirit (though it took a lifetime to come to terms with that). I was never raped, nor violently used, but there are infinite gradations of sexual abuse, from inappropriate speech and unacceptable exposure to invasive touch and acting out, all of which can do irreparable damage. Either way I was left traumatised, and very much alone. I was also left horribly, toxically ashamed.

Despite everything, of course, I still adored him. In a home that was riven by inexplicable angers and jealousies, and later by vicious arguments, he was my one and only source of love. My mother, taking refuge herself in workaholism, withdrew resentfully, blaming me as much as my father. My only attempt to ask for her help was brushed aside impatiently. There was nowhere else to go.

The saving myth was that I was stupid. At some level my father knew what he was doing and he hated himself for it. So it was decided that I wasn't learning anything at the village primary school and should be sent away to a boarding school. At the age of nine, I was duly dispatched to a prep school and stayed there until the money ran out. At this point I took the Eleven Plus examination and, having passed despite my stupidity, was brought back into the home and sent to a grammar school.

The full Greek tragedy kicked in at this point. I was now an increasingly plump and unhappy kid and my father needed to distance himself from me to avoid any repetition of what had happened earlier. The way he managed this was to get drunk, call me into his room, and order me to strip. He would then verbally excoriate me – by which I mean he'd stalk me, walk around me in a circle, snarling, becoming ever more irate, eventually yelling at me, spitting abuse at my fat, pubescent body. Literally unable to defend myself, I stood there, frozen in shame, as he poured the vitriol of his scorn over my young frame. Again and again, while my mother supposedly slept, this travesty of a ritual was played out. In short, I was skinned alive as my father blamed me for what he had done.

And so we became a family of strangers, bound together by shame, but torn apart and shredded beyond all mending. By my fifteenth year the quarrelling was constant, cruel and exhausting. Things began falling apart. My schooling was a disaster and with both my parents drinking, the family business was going down the pan. Eventually, as is the way of tragedy, things came to a head. My mother left home. The week before my father was due to be declared bankrupt, he discovered he had a heart condition and wrote to my mother. She came home.

That night we had a terrible three-way argument. My mother, having vented her bitterness, stormed off to bed, leaving my father and I to turn on each other. I was just old enough to fight back, and for only the second time in his life, my father lashed out and hit me, knocking me to the floor. I went off to my bedroom, and brooded until I heard him on the stairs. He stood at the door. "I'm sorry I hit you," he said. "Let's make it up, old son."

I've looked back on this moment for nearly fifty years. I've talked about it, written about it, and discussed it in therapy. I've approached it in plays and poems, and articles, but I've never been able to wash it away. There are moments in life that feel like fate, when the weight of our inheritance inexorably crushes us, changing our shape and defining our journey. I've wanted it to be different and I've wanted to feel less guilty, but I know that in the circumstances, I couldn't have said or done anything else. As my father stood there, broken and vulnerable, I gathered all the shame of my fifteen years and balled it up into a single word. "Never!"

My father left me without a word and went off to bed. Later, in the middle of the night, my mother woke me, having heard strange noises coming from his room. She wanted me to go and see if he was alright. I told her to wait and went in alone. He was sprawled across the bed, eyes wide open, top lip curled and snarling in death. He'd died of a heart attack and his long nails had clawed at his chest. I tidied him up and told my mother - and the rest of my life began.

~

My father had been the tenant of the pub where I grew up, which meant that, on the day he died, my mother was given a year's notice. At sixteen, I was on my own. There was no money, so my mother got a job behind a bar and arranged for me to take a room in the local town. We packed up a few belongings and left with what we could carry.

What do you do in a moment like this, when your world is imploding and you're on your own? What do you do when you've just lost everything – house and family, integrity and self respect – when you're unable to put a name to what you're feeling, yet trapped in an iron cage of shame and guilt? What I did was automatic. I reached for a symbol, something that would mark what was happening to me, and ground the moment in my reality. For the first time in my life, without words or even feelings, I knew what I had to do. Without giving it the name, I created a ritual.

At the back of the pub there was a flat area where we used to burn off cardboard boxes and garden refuse. I cleared a space and built a pyre of kindling and childhood objects that I'd thrown away: a cowboy hat, a model boat, and my cigarette card collection. I half filled a milk bottle with petrol from the mower. I did all this with unforced solemnity: no veteran by the cenotaph could have held a better silence.

When all was ready, I went to my miserable suitcase and took out my old teddy bear. Fluff was actually a koala bear, made from rabbit fur by an elderly relative. I held him up, and looked him over, running back through the movie of our life together. He'd comforted me through a host of losses, from Great Ormond Street to the shattering of everything. He was bald now, and far from pretty, with one eye missing and a dislocated leg, but I loved him dearly and I always would. He'd been the one constant thing in my chaotic life. When parents and family had let me down, when old friends had died and others moved away, he had remained, unchanging and faithful, as true and dependable as any pet, or friend, or brother.

I took him and silently laid him on the pyre. There were no words to say, no prayers to recite – anything like that would be have been 'pretending'. Instead I trickled the petrol over him, dribbled a long trail, and carefully, respectfully, deliberately lit it. I watched my childhood burn down to nothing. Then I turned and walked away.

~

Ironically, my father had imbued me with a deep if unconscious sense of ritual. Apart from his flirtations with religion and mysticism, he'd been a freemason, which he took extremely seriously. He had also served in the Navy before the war and had an ex-servicemen's sense of ceremonial. Because of all this, he had acquired the habit of investing things with meaning and significance: whether the preparation of a special punch at Christmas, or changing a barrel, or watering the geraniums in the window-boxes, he gave his actions space and dignity – an importance that stayed in the mind.

For instance, whenever he cleaned the beer engines that pumped the ale up from the cellar, my father would invite Harry Palmer, one of the old men of the village, into the public bar to "test the pumps". Having drawn off the cleaning fluid and the water he used to rinse the pipes, he would empty his bucket of slops, then wipe his hands and return to the beer engines. While toothless old Harry watched, licking his lips and beaming, my father would deliberately draw off a long glass of Benskin's best mild ale. He made an initial half-pull on the polished pump-handle, and then another to catch the full pint, which squirted and splashed into the glass leaving a foamy white head. This offering would then be passed over to the waiting Harry who would lift it to the light, take a mouthful and close his eyes before passing an opinion.

To a kid like me the wait was intolerable. Would the ale pass muster? Would Harry give it ten out of ten? Would my father have to start all over and clean the beer engines again? I waited on tenterhooks and hardly noticed the twinkle in Harry's eye as he sank the rest of the pint and placed the glass reverently on the polished wooden counter. "That's what I call a pint o' mild. That'll do nicely."

Looking back on events like these, on Harvest Homes and Christmas lunches, on the formal hours spent reading out loud, and on the precision of every ceremonial action, I can see that it was my father who unwittingly instilled in me the core spirit of ritual. He taught me the value and power of tradition and ceremony, and the deep binding principle of joint intention. But more than that, he gave me a sense of the importance of slowing things down, of creating ritual space out of everyday moments. My father may have hurt me, and ultimately lost me, but he also gave me a priceless gift.

~

There's a solid body of evidence that points to adolescent boys being unable to weep[1]. It's not that they are callous or unfeeling – they can certainly feel – but they are simply unable to cry because their bodies are awash with testosterone. Out on my own at sixteen, I was just such a kid. I needed to grieve, to express my rage, to purge the hurt that I'd unquestionably endured. Above all I needed to break down the wall of shame that surrounded me.

Unable to deal with what had happened to me, I simply shut down. Dry-eyed and shocked out of my body, I did what many boys do – I went numb and denied everything that had happened. In some ways I find it surprising that I didn't take to drugs or kill myself in some adolescent self-initiation, but I survived by a series of flukes and turnings that kept me connected, albeit at the edge.

Firstly, I was blessed by the benign attention of two of my teachers at school. David Shaw and Wendy Carey saw something in me and, quite independently, invited me into their homes. They gave me the odd meal and a sense of tranquillity amidst the storms of my life. The simple rite of breaking bread, of sitting at an evening table in peace and harmony (without any attendant emotional bloodshed) somehow opened up a road of possibilities. It certainly re-established some of my battered trust in humanity. Secondly, they both, in their different ways, introduced me to a world of wide-ranging and intelligent conversation. They talked about travelling to the Greek Islands, or to Russia, and about history and literature. They introduced me to comedians and music, to new authors and life-changing books. Most of all they kept my love of the theatre alive.

I had always been in love with the theatre. At six I had discovered pantomime, and from then on all I wanted was to become an actor. Everything seemed to propel me towards the stage. It was the focused attention, and the creativity of theatrical performance as much as the glitz that captivated me. As a child, looking up at the adults around me in the audience, I noticed a shift from distracted absence to rapt attention and I was fascinated. I quickly grasped that something astonishing was happening, and later understood that I was witness to the very thing that people seemed to hope for but rarely find in church. There was something magical in the depth of the silence and in the flood of emotion that came at the end of a performance when something vital was resolved and the whole audience exhaled in one mighty rush of relief, or joy, or satisfaction.

I took to performance with ease. School plays, trips to Stratford and the West End, and amateur dramatics convinced me, and those around me, that the theatre was where my life would be lived. By my teens I was beginning to see that I could actually become an actor, maybe a good one. The more arts-minded teachers at school encouraged me to think about the theatre as a career path. And later, while my life was disintegrating, my love for the theatre kept me focused on what could have been an ideal life. I yearned for it, I prepared for it, I worked my socks off. It just didn't happen.

Circumstance pointed me down a different road. I vanished into the world of casinos where, within a couple of years, I was frustrated enough to be flexing my muscles as a playwright. Inventing things came easily to me; I'd been practicing denial for most of my life. Writing in the afternoons and going off to the casino in the evenings, I lived in hope of entering what I now knew to be Peter Brook's Holy Theatre, that semi-sacred, liminal space where mysteries took place and magic actually happened. The odd Sunday night performance at the Royal Court, a classy West End agent, and some charming entanglements with theatrical knights left me convinced that I could become a dramatist. The cap looked cool and faintly glamorous, so I wore it.

Fourteen years of unremitting effort and a stack of unproduced plays later, after a year spent on the 'hippy trail' exploring sacred sites from Jerusalem to Varanasi, I found myself commissioned to write a one-man play for the actor Tim Pigott-Smith who had just had a big success in the lead role of a television series called *The Jewel in the Crown*. The play was called Bengal Lancer and followed the spiritual awakening of a young subaltern in the Indian Army before, during and after the First World War. The play went on in Leicester before transferring to London. This was clearly the high watermark of my life to date – the opening of my first play in London – but on the opening night something happened that altered my life, and it wasn't for the better.

In a very real sense I had arrived that night. There would be reviews on television and in the national papers. Doors would start opening and projects would be offered. Yet as I sat in the audience on that first night, surrounded by successful people and in the buzz of anticipation, my world started to implode again. When I shut my eyes, it felt like I was falling.

This particular tumble involved a descent into clinical depression that lasted more than five years. I hid in the casinos, and even got promoted to Pit Boss. I unsuccessfully flirted with drink, and tried unhappily to write my way out of it. I withdrew from my friends, and failed to form anything remotely approaching a healthy relationship. In the hamster cage of my depression I went round and round, increasingly isolated and filled with self-loathing. I hadn't done anything to shift the grief and shame of my childhood experience and it was catching up with me. I got so far down the path of depression that I determined to kill myself.

Some psychologists say that depression is anger turned inwards. I wouldn't argue with that, though I'd add that it is also about an inability to grieve. What professionals tend not to talk about in regard to depression is shame. Long term, chronic or toxic shame paralyses you. It binds up your feelings of rage and sorrow, and freezes you to the spot. It colours your whole life to the point where you don't even know you're in it. The effects of shame are so similar to depression that many of us aren't able to make the distinction. When you are depressed you cease to move, nothing works for you and you grind to a halt. So it can be with shame. My depression or my shame was so pervasive that it filled my whole horizon. Ironically, it was shame that saved my life.

The night I decided to kill myself I was at home in the flat I rented off Borough High Street in Southwark. I had gone through the usual suicide's list of options and decided upon a hot bath and a razor blade as the ideal way to end things. At this point I unconsciously slipped into ritual mode. I went into the bathroom, prepared to lay things out like some kind of Roman patrician. But then I noticed that the room was dirty – not just untidy but really quite grubby. I'd been depressed for so long that I'd not been looking after myself, or my flat. My in-built ritual sensibilities were offended and I prickled with shame. I wondered what would happen when the police broke down the front door. In my mind's eye, I saw a kindly, middle-aged sergeant standing in the hall and distinctly heard the pity and contempt in his voice: "Poor bastard. He lived like a pig."

I felt myself blushing, and hurriedly picked up a cloth and a squeegee bottle of bathroom cleaner. I scrubbed the bath and the sink until they shone, polished the taps and the mirror and took the cleaning equipment out to the kitchen. It looked even worse, so I started to clean the kitchen as well, then the lounge, and then my study. I was just finishing off the bedroom when the telephone rang. It was my shy and rather charming neighbour from the flat upstairs. "For God's sake!" she shouted. "Turn that bloody hoover off. It's three o'clock in the morning!"

The flat was now as shiny as a new pin. I made myself a cup of tea, and sat down on a stool at the squeaky-clean breakfast bar. Sheepishly, I realised that I no longer wanted to kill myself.

~

The following week I took the walk up to my old village, and, soon after that, my frozen life began to thaw. I began to see that I needed to change, that I had a past that I'd somehow hidden from myself. My worn out life of denial and isolation was beginning to crumble but I hadn't yet found the tools to construct a new one.

The one thing I knew was that something had stayed with me. It had been there through the darkest moments with my father; in my reciting and my singing; in my love and exploration of what lay at the very heart of theatre. It was an integral part of me and had even been there when I'd contemplated suicide. It made me feel better and less alone, and it helped me to make sense of my muddle of a life. I needed to find out more about it. I needed to learn.

Chapter Three

Places and Spaces:
The Nuts and Bolts of Ritual

Any ritual is an opportunity for transformation.
To do a ritual you must be willing to be transformed
Starhawk, Writer and Ritualist

You don't have to believe in rituals for them to work.
Professor Michael Norton, Harvard Business School

Catherine Bell, the academic and writer on ritual, once observed that Hindu Brahmins who wanted to explain their spirituality to academics would always take people to see and experience their rituals.[2] That's my aim with this book, to open ritual up and de-mystify it by showing you, and wherever possible taking you through, the rituals that have changed and deepened my life, and that of others. However, I think it might be useful to pause while I explain some of the language we've inherited around the subject. We can then get a sense of the underlying structures in ritual and I can explain some of the basics of ritual practice, as I see them, before exploring different aspects of ritual in more depth in the later chapters.

Sifting the Language – Ritual, Ceremony & Ceremonial

We have a problem in English in that the very word, *ritual*, carries an immense load of meanings and associations. The very mention of ritual can spin some people off into dark little rooms of resentment, or preconception. Others reject the word outright, as either an affront to their religion, or as a threat to the absence of it. Of course, I could go to the Oxford English

Dictionary at this point, and lay down the law, but that would run counter to the ethos of this book, which is (hopefully) anything but proscriptive. With that in mind I'm going to flag up a few key words and try to clarify some of the language that bedevils the subject.

For instance, what is the difference between a ritual and a ceremony? There seems to be no agreement. Victor Turner, the late anthropologist, defined ceremony as maintaining the status quo and ritual as allowing for spontaneity and the shadow.[3] Meanwhile James Roose-Evans, the theatre director and ritualist, would say that ceremonial can be a part of ritual but that ritual cannot be a part of ceremonial.[4] He would then add that ceremonial is concerned with externals while ritual speaks to the internal. I subscribed to this view for many years, but over time my personal experience shifted my view somewhat.

Firstly, it's easy to dismiss ceremony as dull or lifeless when in fact it can be deeply moving. Take the annual ceremony around London's Cenotaph on Remembrance Sunday, or the story of a friend who, during the course of a forty-year military career, rose to become a colonel in a Guards Regiment, an outfit famous for its ceremonial duties. One of his last career tasks was to preside over the lying-in-state of the late Queen Elizabeth the Queen Mother, during which he sat quietly with her flag-draped coffin for a while, before it was moved to the great echoing space of Westminster Hall. As he described this powerful experience, months after the event, he was visibly moved, not just in an old-soldier way, but as a man who had touched something profound, within himself and his culture. Ceremony need not be empty or shallow.

Then again, many of the indigenous cultures I have come to admire and respect for their sacred technologies speak of ceremony and *only* ceremony, hardly mentioning the word ritual at all. I remember one particular wrangle involving a hugely experienced elder who followed a particular Native American tradition, during which I clung to my ritual-is-alive-and-ceremony-is-dead position while she insisted that while ritual might be alright for me and my necromantic buddies she would stick with ceremony, thank you very much.

So, for ease, and with no wish to offend anyone of any particular persuasion or tradition, I propose, for the most part, to use the word *ritual* to refer to activities that bring about a change, and *ceremony* to refer to activities that affirm or reaffirm what already is. I'm going to try and reserve the word *ceremonial* for use around the sometimes empty and proscriptive religious activities that many have come to distrust and reject. My guess is

I'll blur the lines somewhere.

All that still leaves us with the need to say what a ritual actually is, or rather what it does. For the purposes of this book, I would like to suggest the following as a kind of jobbing definition.

A ritual is a symbolic action through which we can give our soul, or psyche, an important message.

Since we first stood up and gazed across the savannah, we have been visual creatures. We communicate in images and think in pictures. So much so that our subconscious, our psyches, or our souls – call it what you will – find it hard to process data. To put it plainly, the soul can't count. It can, however, understand an image. Thus it is that the symbolic action at the heart of a wedding ritual sends a powerful message to the deep psyche/soul of anyone who marries. Not because of the words spoken over the couple or their signature on a legal document, but because of the ritual bestowal or exchange of a wedding ring, which clearly and unambiguously tells a spouse that s/he has entered a different state. There is a before and an after – and the ritual provides the message.

The Gifts of Ritual

Ritual, at its core, can give us clear and potent messages, but it has other important gifts to bestow, amongst which are order, reflection, containment, and communal belonging. These can have life-affirming and potentially life-changing effects, but there is another gift offered by ritual that uniquely gives us a *felt* sense of being alive and present, of 'getting real'. This is the gift of connection. This can be with our fellows, our 'tribe'; or with the environment. It can be with something altogether more nebulous, like a feeling, or an idea – with wonder, for instance, or with an aspect of one's history – or with parts of ourselves we may have disowned or shunned. Then again it can put us in direct contact with the mysterious, the awe-inspiring and the numinous – what the great ethnologist Mircea Eliade used to call The Other and what the archetypal psychologist James Hillman used to call The Invisibles.

Depending upon the individual, connection with these unseen presences and perceptions can, to a greater or lesser extent, support and enrich our inner lives. They tend to appear in our art and dreams, but one of the places where they are most likely to surface is in ritual space.

Be the connection with the wildwood, or with a god, the modern, secular mind is inclined to dismiss this level of connection as superstition or irrational folly, though it is no more irrational than present day economics and financial speculation, both of which are equally grounded in faith and belief – some might even say credulity. That said, notions like The Other and the numinous can be unnerving to our secular mindset. We tend to get the pungent whiff of religiosity which, it must be said, has hurt and shut down many a hungry heart.

In the end, it's a matter of what you bring to a ritual that determines its level of connection. We can speculate about contact with The Other and The Invisibles, we can feel touched and moved by the presence of the environment but in the end, the only certain contact we can have is with a deeper, older, some might say wiser, part of ourselves.

Three Kinds of Ritual

When writing a book on your favourite subject, it's all too easy to dive down inviting rabbit holes and over-complicate things. Having made this mistake, and been dug out by my editors, I've decided to simplify things by reducing the panoply of world ritual to three basic types, which can be defined by their different purposes. For the sake of clarity then, we will be dividing ritual and ceremony into rituals of Continuity, Alignment, and Growth.

Rituals of Continuity

Rituals of Continuity, or we might call them ceremonies, contain the cyclic and recurring rituals of our cultures, the milestones and the celebrations of our lives. Their purpose is to maintain the cohesion of our societies, tribes, and families, to observe the movements of the spheres and to mark the seasons of our cultural narratives and our years. Rituals of continuity include weddings, naming ceremonies and funerals, Remembrance Day ceremonies and family gatherings like Christmas Lunch or Thanksgiving Dinner. They can also include Bonfire Nights, Beltane fires and a host of other annual festivals, and the myriad regular gatherings that occur in between. In the minds of holy men and women the world over, continuity rituals keep the sun coming up every morning.

There was once a young devotee on a tribal reservation in the desert who was tasked by an elder with greeting the dawn. He met the sunrise every day with a great deal of enthusiasm and impassioned chanting. He would then call "Welcome Grandfather" at the very moment the sun rose. Every morning, just as the sun came over the horizon, he heard a gentle rumbling and noticed that the ground beneath his feet shook. He was deeply impressed. After some months of this, his elder brother sneered at him, saying. "You're a fool to follow the old ways. That's not the earth shaking at the sun's arrival. It's the six o'clock train!"

The young devotee went to his teacher in tears. "You made a fool of me," he cried. "It wasn't the earth moving at all. It was just a rusty old train."

"Ah", smiled his teacher. "But have you noticed, the sun is still coming up every morning!"

Rituals of Alignment

Sometimes we get out of kilter with the world. Things go wrong and our stars seem to be against us. It's as if there were a flow to life, a natural tide that carries us and supports us. The Taoists of China say that we should yield to this current calling it *Wu Wei*, the Watercourse Way, of inaction and surrender. Others, pagans for instance, would think of it as an alignment with nature, the seasons, or the great cycles of existence. In the West this goes against our relatively new sense of individuality and self-determination. We see surrender as failure and often find ourselves swimming against this flow of life. In doing so we can feel oppressed or battle against the odds, step out of integrity, experience tragedy, or fall ill with some strange, mysterious illness. At such a moment – when a clinical psychologist might reach for the formulary and the pills, a shaman might say that you were out of alignment with the spirits and prescribe a ritual to restore some kind of harmony within your soul. The Dagara medicine man, Malidoma Somé, calls these *radical* rituals. They are highly evocative, often effective and indisputably powerful rites of healing and change. In secular terms we might say that they help to re-balance us psychologically, to restore us to a kind of emotional equilibrium in which we are more comfortable 'in our skins'.

Rituals of alignment can include grief rituals, rebirthing rituals, and atonement rituals (which are only half-jokingly referred to as 'at-one-ment' rituals). Of necessity they tend to have a degree of healing involved in them, and can be life-changing events. While rituals of alignment, like continuity rituals, can involve whole communities, they can also be very private affairs, witnessed by no more than a friend or supporter, and still bring about a radical adjustment of a person's view of themselves and the world. Separation rituals also come under this heading.

Rituals of Growth

Throughout the journey of our lives we find ourselves breaking through to new levels of attainment, and maturity. In our culture, especially when we are young, we tend to do this rather arbitrarily through self-defined adventures, and peer-led 'dares', which are risky and occasionally fatal, and may leave us damaged and scarred rather than welcomed into the next circle of adulthood. Traditional cultures are more careful of their young and provide rites of passage, intensely supervised challenges and genuine ordeals designed to bring young people through to a recognizable and respected maturity. In fact, indigenous peoples, wherever they remain untainted by western mores, tend to provide regular initiations throughout life for both sexes, from adolescence through to elderhood.

A rite of passage is actually one of the core rituals of humankind. Practically universal in tribal societies, it is largely absent from our culture, to our great loss. The French ethnographer, Arnold Van Gennep, divided rites of passage into three distinct phases based on the idea of the *limen* or threshold[5]: they were *pre-liminal, liminal*, and *post-liminal*, a neat poetic triad which has become mangled over the years, so that it comes down to us most commonly as *Separation, Ordeal* and *Return*. It's a clumsy nomenclature in the hands of literalists, who tend to overdo the *Ordeal* phase in the name of machismo. I prefer to use a mixture of Van Gennep and Victor Turner's terms, which gives us the everyday yet clearly distinct phases of *Separation, Transition* and *Incorporation*. These three words are useful to us in that they give us a basic outline for any ritual we may care to unpick or analyse, or for that matter create.

Initiations are not entirely absent from our Western lives, of course. In later life, as philosophical and spiritual musings impinge more and more on our consciousness, we can find ourselves going on a pilgrimage, embarking on a meaningful journey, or entering a phase of intense learning, from which we move on with a new sense of ourselves, having shed our old skin and grown into another: separation – transition – incorporation.

Vision quests, death lodges and various rites of passage are all typical growth rituals, as are retreats and sabbaticals, walkabouts, pilgrimages, and initiations into closed societies such as Freemasonry.

While each of these categories has a distinct flavour, and makes very different demands upon us, it's also true to say that, given the complexity of our inner worlds, we can find ourselves in more than one of these general categories at any one time. Rituals are multifarious and layered events. I think it's best not to think of rituals as being readily broken down into 'Ten Steps', or 'Five Golden Rules', or some such formulaic template. We may divide ritual into types for ease of understanding, but the fact remains that, simple as they may be, they can also be extraordinarily complex in both form and performance. At its best, ritual is an art form, every bit as exacting and rigorous as dance or theatre, or the other performative arts to which it gave rise.

Spaces & Places – Ritual, Liminal & Sacred Space

Having determined what a ritual is, and decided what kind we might want to do, we need to find a place to do it. Of course, we could say that ritual space is just the location where a ritual happens, but as we are coming to see with this subject, it's more complicated than that.

The ancients used to speak of the *temenos* or sacred precinct, which was an area separated from day-to-day existence and dedicated to the gods. In our post-modern civilization we don't have the luxury of such places (unless we are attached to a formal religious community), but we can set aside a space, *in time*, to be dedicated to ritual or ceremonial activity.

Peter Brook, the theatre director, wrote about the 'Empty Space' that invites a drama into being.[6] It doesn't need to be elaborate, or to have red plush seats and a proscenium arch to do its job. It merely needs to be a space, which begs the question, what happens next? So it is with ritual. The towering gothic cathedrals and temples that our forebears were so awed by, with their strictly prescribed areas and architectural hierarchies, are no more necessary to the creation of true ritual than a fairy palace or a procession of priests. All we need to make good ritual is an appropriate space – a dedicated ritual space – ideally one that doesn't impinge on anyone else's.

And now we start to layer in levels of complexity. Firstly, depending on the purpose or depth of the ritual, we might need to make sure that the space affords us some seclusion or privacy, that it is safe, and that it is free of clutter, both physical and psychic. Secondly, we can dedicate or solemnise our chosen space before we enter it, thus making it sacrosanct for the duration of our ritual; in a sense defining it temporarily as sacred space. This is more than mere pomp. By declaring or delineating such a space, we have defined a temenos, a space in which something transformational can happen.

This brings us to a third level within ritual space that is harder to define, until such time as we experience it. It lies at the heart of a ritual's power to contain and change. This is a place's 'threshold quality' of ambiguity and disorientation – its *liminality*. In liminal space you are likely to find yourself stepping away from the normal rules, constraints and hierarchies of society, and suspending your normal thinking and behaviour. As a consequence we find ourselves 'in a very different place'. This may be associated with a physical space, as were many of the sacred chambers and henges of our long-lost past, but it is also, crucially, a place in the heart, a spot that holds deep feeling and openness, which supports possibilities and transformation. Such is the mysterious, melting – we might even say magical – quality of liminal space.

Communitas

The creation of a ritual space and of liminality allows for another phenomenon, which Victor Turner[7] called *communitas*. This refers to either a community that has shed its structures and hierarchies, or to the very spirit of community itself. Setting aside anthropology's preoccupation with 'structure and anti-structure', we are left with something immensely important that sits at the heart of ritualising and indeed at the very heart of being human. In our modern world, the performance of rituals allows for a common experience in which people enter liminal space together. In doing this the walls of our social preconceptions are broken down, whilst simultaneously moving us from internal isolation and grandiosity to a kind of 'ritual belonging'. It also – I would say exceptionally – brings us to a wholly natural if temporary humility. Communitas allows us to experience belonging and modesty in the same breath, preparing us for greater social responsibility, and in our increasingly uncaring world, opening us to the gifts of humility: empathy, understanding, and kindness.

Paraphernalia, Tools & Ritual Objects

Amongst the questions I'm most commonly asked by people interested in doing a ritual is, "What kind of things do I need to bring?"

Most of the rituals I'm writing about tend to be simple and uncluttered by accretions of stuff, though we'll later be seeing that *mess* in ritual can be surprisingly beneficial. After twenty-odd years of ritualising, my 'ritual-box' contains surprisingly little: some incense and smudge, a penknife, feathers, a pot of assorted beads, lengths of cloth and a ball of red string. I also possess a cigar box, which is partly filled with small objects and gifts. In my kind of ritualising I have no need of a wand and whenever I have dressed for the part I have usually felt more foolish than otherwise – or worse, triggered someone's fears around religion and/or magic. I do however expect and ask people to make ritual objects, in ritual space, either as offerings or as ritual 'makings' (objects that an anthropologist would probably call fetishes) that serve in different parts of a ceremony. These can be beautiful, and richly worked, but having been used, they invariably get burned or buried or left to decay in nature.

Generally speaking I would say that the less paraphernalia we bring to ritual the better. That said, I'm also clear that many rituals call for meaningful objects to be brought to them, and that ritual 'makings' are invariably invested with lots of feeling. Human beings tend to invest even ordinary objects with significance. The important thing is to strike a balance between investing things with meaning on the one hand and avoiding an often unconscious, inherited Puritanism on the other. It's also a matter of aesthetics, which I've come to realise are hugely important in ritual.

So, whilst acknowledging our need for meaningful objects in our rituals, I think it's also important to only use things that are appropriate to the occasion; otherwise we can find ourselves focusing on the object rather than the activity and drifting into empty show. Some years back, I was working with Ron Pyatt, who taught me more about aesthetics and appropriateness in ritual than anyone else I know. We were about to begin a commencement ritual, at the beginning of a workshop, and Ron asked for a bowl to hold some water. One of our circle dashed off, only to return with a rather beautiful goblet inset with semi-precious stones, a real 'holy grail' of a goblet. He offered it solemnly to Ron saying, "This chalice has been to every one of the seven sacred sites of Britain."

Ron looked at it, and then at the circle around him – people who at that point he didn't know from Adam. Finally he spoke.

"Have you got a Tupperware bowl?"

Who Should Run a Ritual?

Human ritual is thought by some archaeologists to have started when people sought to bring good fortune to the hunt[8], or to propitiate the darkness that surrounded them. Whether they were facing a thunderstorm, a forest, or a sabre-toothed tiger, people needed to feel safe. They also needed to express and contain their feelings of anxiety or fear. At this point I imagine that someone who was particularly aware of what was going on around them had an intuition about what to do, and stepped forward to lead the group in a kind of proto-ritual. They did a good job and were given extra food for their trouble.

As time went by, those whose rituals best served the group's needs became recognised and powerful individuals who stood next to the leader as the group grew into a tribe, the tribe grew into a people, and the people grew into a nation.

These intuitives – we can call them priests now – developed their ceremonies as the group's circumstances changed. In time the ideas became religions and the ceremonies lost their immediacy. Today, after centuries of religious strife, the rise of science and the horror of modern warfare, many people have rejected their priesthoods out of hand, along with their religions and their ceremonies. However we are left with a ritual-sized gap in our lives that leaves us feeling bereft. Babies and bathwater...

All this begs some serious questions. "Do we need a priest to hold our rituals?" "Can anyone hold a ritual?" and "What does the job of holding ritual entail?" While many clerics would claim a 'divine right' to mediate, my sense is that it's all about choice and necessity. We wouldn't dream of holding our own wedding ceremony, for instance, though we might perform a ritual that privately bound us to one we loved for life. The first is a public act that needs 'holding' and a call to witness, while the second is an intimate declaration of love and devotion. We can easily hold some ceremonies and rituals ourselves, while others call for someone to 'officiate' or run it for us. This person may or may not be, and certainly doesn't have to be, a priest.

So what is it that a priest, or ritual leader is doing that makes them necessary and occasionally still indispensable? The key word that arises here is *mediation* (which comes from the Latin *mediatus, to be placed in the middle*). The role of the priesthood of old was to mediate with their gods, to stand between the community and The Other; be that a shaman with the spirits, a priest with his saints, or a high priestess with her god. In a religious context this mediation is seen as essential. It allows for the priestess to intercede on behalf of her tribe, and conversely, to translate any *message* handed down by the divine.

In a strictly secular context we no longer need to call on the spirits or beg the gods to spare us (though we may still wish to invoke The Invisibles, however we might imagine them), but there are associated priestly functions that may still be necessary, not the least of which is *holding*. I first came across the term *holding* in a psychotherapeutic context and was deeply suspicious. However, the more I came to see people's vulnerability in liminal space – in workshops, retreats and rites of passage – the more I came to appreciate a ritualist's skill in holding a group emotionally. This seemed to involve throwing an envelope of care and attention around the whole group, as a parent would a child, or as a great performer would an audience. It's actually an act of caritas, of love.

Sad to say, many of us have been to religious ceremonies where the envelope of love has *not* been extended, and felt the cold slap of indifference. As we move off into creating our own forms of ceremony, there remains a need for persons of understanding and heart to take us through some passages of the soul. We can delegate the task to the whole group, or hand it over to an individual, someone who might stand as a ritual elder, or at least hold the envelope.

The Stages of Ritual

We can now turn to a ritual template, a kind of checklist that we can run through when contemplating any ritual. This template shows the steps that lead to the construction and 'performance' of a safe and solid ritual which, like a meaningful play or a film, picks you up at one point and sets you down later at another. It is important to understand that, like a play, even an apparently improvised ritual has its own inner logic, that it obeys the rules of ritual architecture. These rules may not be obvious but they are most certainly there. In fact if you choose to unpick any ritual you will probably find these precepts lying in there somewhere. You might think of them as the five essentials of ritual construction. They are:

1. Purpose & Planning – Setting an Intention

This is an indispensable part of any ritual, in which we need to set our intention. Setting and holding an intention is the fundamental premise of any ritual and it is wise to ask ourselves a few searching questions before we begin: "What kind of ritual is this going to be?" and, perhaps most importantly of all, "What do we want to achieve in this ritual?" This saves us from floundering around later, trying to make sense of a ritual that, like a badly constructed play or cake, has lost shape and gone flat. In considering our intention we need to become clear about the purpose of our ritual and what has moved us to perform it. Only when you have determined and clarified your intention can you start on the planning of the Who, What, and How of the thing.

2. Preparation & Logistics

This can be the most time-consuming part of any ritual. It necessarily includes the gathering and preparation of materials, ritual objects, food and drink, and the organisation of timings, music, stories, or poetry, if you choose to use them. You might, for instance, need to build a shrine, or set up an altar, dig a pit, prepare a fire, or carry gallons of water up a hill.

The preparation time before a ritual tends to be a time of creativity and fellowship. We develop friendships at such times which, because they are forged in the intensity of ritual, can last a lifetime. I have friends that I met during rituals over twenty years ago, friends that I know I can call on to this day.

While not a full-on public performance, any ritual *is* performed, so it is often worthwhile to rehearse any music or chants that you have chosen. If you are being joined by others and chanting it is especially helpful to teach them the chant and rehearse beforehand. It allows people to feel comfortable, and gets them beyond the "do-I-stand-or-do-I-kneel" place that can embarrass and disconnect people of a Christian or post-Christian background. Rehearsing can be an enjoyable activity, which brings people together and makes them feel a part of things rather than an outsider or observer.

Sometimes in all the excitement of preparing the space and the activities of a ritual we overlook the one thing we really do need to prepare - ourselves. Before we undertake a ritual therefore, it's good to do a check-in with ourselves and see how we might be doing. Are there any intuitions that I might like to fold into my ritual, or any inspired thoughts or images that might make a difference?

3. Opening & Invocation

Now you have prepared your ritual, you are ready to start – but where do you begin? Every human story needs a beginning, as does a ritual, if it is to be effective. The beginning sets the tone and the direction of the proceedings, allowing you to bring the space 'alive', and follow your intention.

You might want to use something to purify or clean the space: smoke, salt, and water are traditionally used to prepare a ritual space by clearing away negative associations or thought forms (or spirits or ghosts).

Sometimes it is good to make an invocation. While historically this was often done to invoke The Other – to awake or notify the spirits, saints or gods – in a secular ceremony, this need not be a religious act so much as a declaration of presence. You are merely opening the proceedings, bringing the space alive, and this is best done orally. Keeping things in your head doesn't sit well with the act of ritualising, which calls for you to be present. Alternatively, you might like to light a candle, or point towards the four cardinal directions, North, East, South and West, defining your connection to the cosmos. On a couple of occasions, when a ritual has been called for without any time to prepare, I have simply begun a ritual by concentrating hard on my intention and then clapping my hands: once, twice, three times.

4. Action and Expression – the Heart of the Ritual

This brings you to the *doing* part of your ritual, in which you perform the actions that follow through on your declared intention. This could be a declaration, a renunciation, or a meeting with a forgotten or shunned part of yourself. Sometimes it is a dramatic event, at other times the opening of a slow but profound realisation.

At this stage the more direct and authentic the action(s) the better. Even the pouring of a libation onto the ground, or the lighting of a joss stick can have considerable significance once the space has been prepared and properly opened.

In a live ritual space, with all its liminality, it is worth concentrating on a couple of simple points. Firstly, it helps to keep the proceedings plain and simple. If you feel moved to speak out loud, do so simply and clearly in as wholehearted a way as possible. Remember, this is between you and The Other or, depending on where you are on the secular-to-sacred spectrum, between you and your psyche, or your soul.

Secondly it is important to hold to your intention. Interesting and exciting things can happen, or occur to you, in ritual space, and it is good to bear your ritual purpose in mind, so that you can avoid distractions and navigate your way to a satisfactory close. It might even be good to have an object to hand, a little ritual thingamabob you've made to stand as a reminder of what you are actually here for.

Even in the simplest of rituals you may find yourself deeply moved or full of unexpected feeling (this is why it's good to have someone there with you). Alternatively you might find yourself getting bored and frustrated, which can be a message in itself. On more than one occasion I've had to ask myself, "Okay. What's going on behind this irritation?" Either way, once you have authentically opened and begun a ritual it is usually the case that the ritual begins to work on *you* too.

Usually, no matter how inexperienced, you find yourself instinctively knowing what to do. It is as if you have tapped into some old folk memory. You say and do exactly the right things, and the ritual evolves and unfolds as your natural creativity and ritual-presence kicks in. You just need to trust yourself.

5. Closure & Grounding

A meaningful ritual is like a fire – you need to be careful around it. This means setting it properly, containing it, and ultimately closing it down. The closure is especially important. A medicine teacher or shaman would say that by starting a ritual, by simply standing in ritual space and announcing yourself, you make the spirits aware of your presence. Spirits in the West, having been ignored for so long, can be intrusively curious. It is therefore good practice to shut down the energy evoked and carefully close any emotional or psycho-spiritual doors we may have opened.

In your ritual you might like to consider how you come to a gracious close. At its most direct and literal you can simply say that you are finishing now that you have completed your ritual and that you are coming to a close. A closing gesture, the putting out of a candle or smudge stick, or another three claps of the hands, can also serve to create a clear and definite ending.

Why is this so necessary? In rituals we alter our state by simply entering ritual space and 'beginning' our process. This can leave us wistful and vague in a kind of semi-dream state. If we don't create another change of state, we can literally get stuck in liminal space. This can cause problems when we drive home or turn on the computer. It's worth remembering in the hours immediately after a ritual that the little red light winking in your car is a sign that you are running out of petrol, and not a message from the underworld. In the same vein, after your ritual, you might like to ground yourself. Go for a brisk walk, take a swim, eat a hearty meal or find another way to bring yourself back to the here and now. If nothing else a splash of cold water on the face helps to 'break the spell' of ritual, leaving you clear-headed for whatever you want to do next.

Tidying up is an important part of ritual practice. I tend to collect all the sweepings and unused materials from the creative part of any ritual and ceremonially dispose of them in nature after the ritual ends. This helps me to ground myself, and offload any other person's unexpressed feelings that can stick like burrs. I've come to think of it as spiritual hygiene.

Devotion, Sacrifice, Offering & Exchange

I spent a lot of time in my younger days exploring various religions and was drawn to eastern philosophies, especially the various sects of Buddhism, and to Taoism, but somehow – at least as they were packaged back then – they seemed to lack something important to me. What I came to realise was that I still yearned for something that philosophy alone couldn't supply, and that was a focus for my sense of *devotion*. Perhaps this was simply two thousand years of piety tugging me towards some kind of observance, but I needed to express something profound. In my case, I think it was a mixture of love and gratitude.

I don't think I'm alone in this. Throughout history people have made sacrifices, giving something of themselves with every offering. It's easy to think of them as superstitious or opiated by religion, but they are neither coerced nor conned. In rituals of all kinds, when allowed or asked, people willingly bring their offerings and their gifts – often far more than might be expected. This tells me that numbers of us are seeking connection and that the instinctive human urge to give has as much to do with sacrifice and offering as dread or fear. On that basis I'm including sacrifice and the idea of mutual exchange as an integral part of ritual.

There's a widespread indigenous notion of collective indebtedness and exchange. Tribal peoples from Meso-America to the South Sea Islands see everything as ultimately contributing to the unending continuum of creation while, at the same time, they feel beholden for the priceless gift of life. As living creatures, and a part of this continuum, we are therefore called upon to express our indebtedness to life, which itself gives us life.

There was, and is, an ancient ritual called the *Potlatch*, meaning the Giveaway, which was evolved by the tribes of the Pacific North West. This is a wonderful yet simple metaphor for this infinitely complex idea of collective indebtedness. Each person is asked to contribute to the circle according to what they can give, and to withdraw from the circle according to what they might need. This was a great leveller, of course, and was deemed an alternative form of exchange. So much so that it was declared illegal by the authorities of Canada and the US, who thought of it as dangerous, wasteful and contrary to civilised notions of capitalism.

This puts our old idea of sacrifice in a very different light. What we are looking at now is a form of mutual exchange that feeds a virtuous circle of gift and acknowledgement. Out can go any ideas of horror and bloodletting, and in can come a sense of belonging, maintained by mutual gift and gratitude. In contemporary rituals, this gives us an opportunity to express our sense of gratitude and our inherent creativity by making objects, investing them with all our craft and compassion, and giving them back (often in altered form) to the world of which we are a part.

A Personal Practice – Making Blót

Gradually, in seeking to adapt and bring the old ways back home, I developed a small ritual practice, which I call 'making blót'[9]. This brings together an aspect of my Viking heritage (the word blót comes from the old Norse, blótan, meaning to sacrifice) and this indigenous concept of collective indebtedness. While making blót began for me as a way of 'saying grace', of consciously acknowledging the food I was eating, it quickly deepened to the point where I was giving blót for a beautiful morning or on the way home after an important meeting. I don't make a big thing of it – it often involves no more, indoors, than the placing of a bead or a button in a corner or, outdoors, pressing a tiny rolled-up poem or a bead into the ground. Some might see this as primitive superstition, while others might think of me as seeking to live harmoniously in the world. Either way it involves the gift of some little token I've created, or at the very least, a man-made object, a discreet expression of gratitude, which brings me a daily sense of reciprocal connection, and an oddly disproportionate amount of peace. I certainly have a lot to be grateful for.

Chapter Four

Finding a Tribe
Community and Ritual

Ritual is necessary for us to know anything ...
Ken Kesey

A s I write this, I'm sitting above a lake in Maine. My wife, Juliet, has given me the most astonishing birthday present – a month-long holiday on a New England pond – which fulfils a long-held fantasy of American summers spent writing, canoeing and pottering. Our little clapboard cottage on Albion Pond is all I could ever have wished for. A bed overlooking the water, simple rooms, and a deck with steps leading down to a jetty where a canoe is moored. This morning I'm thinking about how far I've come since I started my life's practice of ritual by burning my teddy bear, and tentatively placing those stones on my dear friends' graves.

Meaningful ritual is now a conscious part of my life. Every morning over here I rise and go down to the water, which more often than not is wrapped in a delicate tissue of mist. I climb into the canoe and set off towards the opposite shore where, having paddled furiously to build up speed, I drift in silence towards a solitary pine tree that stands out above the haze. As the slow sun burns off the mist, I sit in my canoe, absorbed by the stillness, and the sight above me. The lone pine is the roost of a pair of eagles: white-headed and imperious, American bald eagles.

Over the last fortnight, they seem to have accepted me as some weird yet harmless species of amphibian that has neither the grace of an otter nor the bulk of a moose. For my part, I've given up on pictures and take no notes. I simply sit there looking up at the eagles as they look down at me, incurious and preening in the growing light. One morning, early on, when the larger of the two, the female, looked irked by my arrival, and ready to take flight, I began to hum, just a random riff, with no particular tune or shape. It seemed to have an effect because she settled, shrugged and returned to her preening.

Since then, most mornings, I hum my arrival, and once or twice I've sung a sad song, for no better reason than that I was feeling sad. Then, more often than not, I lapse into what the Shakers over at Sabbathday Lake would call companionable silence. This little communion can go on for up to forty minutes, and probably has more to do with the time it takes for an eagle's wings to dry out than any talent or quality of mine. It usually ends with the female flying off, and me acknowledging an ever-deeper level of gratitude. I make blót, dropping a glass bead into the water while mumbling some heartfelt words, and return to the jetty and the cottage.

The point here is not that my morning ritual deepens my experience of life, which it does, or that it brings about some radical transformation, which it doesn't – it's just a maintenance ritual akin to those our ancestors performed to greet the dawn or honour the turning of the seasons. No, the point here is that my ritual is *conscious*. I've chosen to do it and created it with a full intention of communing with the more-than-human world of nature, and of giving thanks for the remarkable experience (for one of my bloodline) of being alive, over sixty, and relatively sane.

During the last twenty years or more, I have learned to consciously create ritual wherever and whenever possible. By developing a series of symbolic practices, I have come to a point where I can manage things life throws at me and feel better 'in my skin'. I've found a way to reduce the aching sense of separateness, of somehow not belonging, that used to plague me, and to satisfy that part of me that has always yearned for something deeper. That's a big shift from my time in the casinos, so I need to briefly take you back there to tell the tale of how I emerged from isolation into community, a first step on the road to living a consciously ritualised life.

~

One evening, back in 1989, I was at work in the casino. The telephone rang and I was told that my closest friend, Dave Frank, had died of a heart attack in Miami, at the age of fifty. As I held the phone, I remembered the last time I had seen him. We had argued, bitterly. I had taken exception to his drinking and he had returned to America without us making it up. Now, as I put the phone down, a small bomb of grief exploded behind my eyes.

A year or two earlier, I had found myself on a travel-writing assignment in New York where I heard about an organization called Al-Anon, ACoA[10]

56

for the families, and specifically the surviving children, of alcoholics. On returning home, I discovered that Al-Anon's UK headquarters was close enough to where I lived for me to pass it every time I went to the launderette. I ignored it assiduously.

Now, as my feelings around Dave's death and our parting mixed horribly with memories of my father's death, the unobtrusive sign on Al-Anon's front door caught the light every time I walked past. One night, when the churning shame and grief became unbearable, I found myself walking into my first Al-Anon meeting. It was like a haven in a storm.

I immediately felt a kinship and a sense of belonging. Week after week I would sit in a circle, head bowed in shame, as I listened to the stories of others who were dealing with the effects of growing up with similarly alcoholic and often abusive parents. Gradually, as I began to realise that I wasn't the only one recovering from my 'problem', I started to recount my own story. As the comforting repetitions of naming and respectful acceptance broke through my shame I started the long slow journey of exploring, re-evaluating and literally re-covering my denied and buried past. I began to see the huge benefit of what was in all but name a ritual process with weekly readings, agreed rules of speaking and behaving, and even a ritual closure, of hand-holding in a circle and chanting a mantra. As a child I had desperately needed structure and consistency in my life. Now I had it, and I saw that the underpinning of that consistency was ritual and community.

My first 'sharing', in the basement of a church off London's Marylebone High Street, came out of my sense of shock and loss at Dave's death. Afterwards I was invited to join a group of men at a local café where the conversation centred almost exclusively on a poet from Minnesota called Robert Bly, who was giving talks and workshops for men, which people were calling men's work, in which he explored the naivety of modern men, our lack of 'wildness' and our inability to feel or express feelings, especially grief.

By the end of that month I had read Bly's book, *Iron John*[11], twice and bought as many of his tapes as I could find. He seemed to be speaking directly to my experience, and I wasn't alone. Amongst the men at ACoA meetings there was a buzz of excitement around Bly, who made a point of acknowledging his own 'wound' at the hands of his father's drinking.

Bly was one of a group of authors who were exploring men's issues such as numbness, the father-son relationship, and intimacy. One day another book arrived in the post. It was John Lee's *The Flying Boy*[12], which in the simplest, most accessible language, touched me as deeply as any book ever had. For the first time I saw how my dysfunctional background had led me directly to a point where I was isolated and stuck, unable to express what felt like overwhelming grief.

As I sat in the café listening to the men around me sharing their excitement and curiosity about men's work, I was acutely aware that I didn't have the money to travel to America to take part in one of Robert Bly's already famous men's conferences, nor to attend one of John Lee's workshops on grief or intimacy. At which point a coincidence came whooping up over the horizon.

One of the men I had come across through ACoA, Peter, was putting together a conference for people in recovery. John Lee's name leapt out at me from the list of speakers. A short while later I found myself sitting in the audience, listening to John Lee. His direct thrust and good ol' boy, country style was compelling, and his moving stories rang true at every level, especially when he spoke about his relationship with his alcoholic father and the need for men to sort themselves out emotionally. He also spoke of men's groups in America where men gathered regularly in 'ritual space' to share their feelings, reduce isolation, and learn how to be around each other without either fighting or putting each other down.

There's a bit of the revivalist in John Lee – he was once a Baptist preacher – and at the end of his first session he couldn't help but sell a little snake oil, or so I thought at the time. Just as the intense applause was dying down, John put his hand up and called out in his deep southern drawl. "There's some fellas down here who are lookin' to set up a ritual men's group here today. I advise any man who wants to change his life to come on down and meet these guys." Curiosity overcame me and despite my cynicism, I found myself joining a group of men down at the front. A week later I was sitting in a circle, listening to six other men as they wrestled with their demons too. It felt like coming home.

That first night we quietly wept together as, one by one, we spoke of our relationships with our fathers. Some had been beaten, others ignored or abandoned, some abused and others let down in all the ways that fathers in our culture fail their boys. Over the next couple of years, as we deepened our fellowship and got to know each other better, we explored all sorts of topics. We were seven very different men with varying degrees of education and assorted forms of addiction, failure and loss in our past, as well as a rich spread of talents and potentials. And what actually held us together – as our differences became all the more apparent, was a growing love and understanding of ritual.

Every time we met, for instance, we would drum, ragged at first and gradually tighter, as a way of ritually arriving in the group. The hand-on-skin contact, the energy released, and the timelessness of the rhythms; the deep heart-pounding beat of the dun-dun, the hi-hat tap of the Levantine dumbeg, or the slap and boom of the West African djembe – all brought us into our bodies no matter how heady and disconnected our conversation before we sat down. Every time. After fifteen or twenty minutes of drumming we were ready to both speak and listen. The distracted talk after a day's work can leave you more separate than together, while a story, or a poem, no matter how good or well meant, can miss its mark, but a session of drumming can remind you of your humanity like nothing else. Over the months, the drumming helped us to build a container for whatever else needed to happen.

Any conscious act of ritual can create and bind a group together, and the more of these acts, the deeper the attachment and sense of belonging. The simple lighting of a candle, as long as it has meaning for the one who lights it, can help to focus the most distracted group of self-obsessed egos, while the regular reading of a poem as a way of opening a space for conversation, or the recitation of a myth, and an associated act to embody it, can create a commonality of experience that can forge bonds of friendship and understanding unlike any other. We experimented as a group with many such rituals. In fact, this group was to break up after a few years, but my experiences, and the unforgettable ritual moments we created together, will stay with me, as will my memories of the men involved, for the rest of my life.

~

For about a year, one of the men in our group, who was divorced and trying to build a ground-breaking medical practice, found it hard to find a child minder on the nights of our meetings. As a consequence, he asked to bring his son along to the men's group. Little Josh would have just turned six when he started coming along. He loved the drumming, and though he never sat in the circle he would always beat time, banging away on anything that made a satisfactory noise. As our conversation continued, little Josh would curl up under one of the chairs happily surrounded by growly men until such time as his dad lifted him up to carry him home.

Then came the week of Josh's birthday. At the previous meeting we had decided that for this special evening, Josh would be nominated as 'ritual elder' and given complete control of the proceedings. As befitted any boy who had achieved a full seven years, he would be calling the shots for as long as he could keep awake.

It was the most delightful chaos. There was drumming, lots of drumming, and Josh sat in the circle with his own drum, bashing away with the best of us. Then there was lemonade, and crisps, and jelly, and cake and more lemonade and more crisps and still more drumming. And then we played games. And Josh got to tell us exactly what he wanted us to do. And we all did exactly as we were told. And at last little Josh's eyes began to droop, and no matter how much he wanted to keep awake he couldn't, and eventually we crooned him a lullaby as he curled up under his dad's chair, with a big-boy's smile all over his face.

Next, as agreed, one of us brought out a paper bag into which we had all placed a photograph of ourselves taken at about seven years of age. The photos were tipped out into the centre of the circle and shuffled around. We were then invited, one by one, to pick up a photo that wasn't our own and describe the boy we saw, without any naming or guessing of names. As we went round the circle the energy slowed and dropped as each photo revealed a sad and lonely kid. More than one of us wept as we heard the descriptions of ourselves as neglected, forgotten, or, in some cases, already lost and abused young boys.

~

One of the guys in the group, Paul, was also interested in understanding the mechanics of what constituted a good ritual. We were soon driving out to the Surrey woods on summer's evenings, practicing what we had gleaned from books and tapes. A lone walker would have seen two earnest men, deep in conversation, holding smoking bundles of herbs, addressing the four cardinal points of the compass, or simply standing there, drinking in the evening and gaining a sense of the responsive nature of the phenomenological world around us: two country lads, long cut off from the land yet finding their way back home again. Paul was also inspired by Robert Bly, and it was through him that I found myself attending my first full-scale men's conference, when Robert Bly came to teach in England.

There's no way to explain what it feels like to go to your first men's gathering, except to say that it can be terrifying. In my case it didn't help that the event was taking place at an ex-boarding school whose very brickwork whispered institutional abandonment, threat and violence. That said, I soon settled in and found my feet. I learned a lot in the teaching sessions, and the culminating ritual, with its midnight walk across frosty fields towards a welcoming fire, was to stay with me for years. However, it was Robert Bly I had come to see and I wasn't to leave disappointed. In the closing ritual I found myself face to face with him for the first time, and it changed my life.

Bly would still have been in his sixties at the time. Tall and rangy with wispy, white hair and a penchant for embroidered weskits, he challenged the room by his very presence; throwing out assertions and opinions like a great Catherine Wheel, mischievously sparking off debate and downright contradiction at every turn.

The Hindus call it *Darshan*. It's a kind of ritual blessing where followers line up and the teacher makes momentary contact with each one of them in turn. In the case of some gurus it is all people turn up for; any teaching *per se* is incidental. The undoubted gift of Darshan can be dispensed through a loving look or a motherly hug or a couple of intuitive words. In Bly's case, and I was to learn of him doing this again and again over the years, he would relax, settle back into his profound intuition and trust himself to say the right thing in ritual space as yet another face swam into view in front of him. He looked me in the eye and simply said, "I see you as an old man …"

To say this shook me was an understatement. This towering old man with his funny waistcoats and his bag of books had simply turned my life upside down. "I see you as an old man." It stayed with me for months like a zen koan, or a loose tooth that had to be worried until it finally fell out. You see, I had always believed that I was going to die young. I simply wasn't prepared for the possibility that I might actually have to live *a whole life!* Hitting my thirties had been shock enough but here I was looking at forty, and Bly was suggesting that I might live to become old. Night after night, working at the casino, I worried this loose tooth, and then it fell out. I realised that I wasn't living my own life at all. I was living the life that my parents had wanted me to live – their life.

"Whatever you do, don't give up your job," my mother used to say whenever I floated the idea of travelling or changing my life. I had been born into a place where people got drunk and played cards late at night, and here I was working in a place where – well, a place where people got drunk and played cards late at night. It was safe and familiar, but it wasn't a life. Bly, Lee, and others in the nascent men's movement, had introduced me to a world of creativity and fulfilment, of authenticity and risk. My ritual experience in recovery and men's groups had begun to give me a sense of myself as someone other than the shrinking man who was, for some as yet unknown reason, afraid to be seen and afraid to take his rightful place in the world.

That summer, I won a poetry competition, the Piccadilly Poets Competition for spoken poetry. On my way home from work I passed a print shop in Borough High Street, which had a framed picture on an easel in the centre of its window display. The picture was of a single floating feather and beneath it there was a caption, which read, "Leap and the net will appear." That evening I went into work at the casino and gave notice. "Leap and the net will appear," I thought. So I leapt. And it didn't.

Chapter Five

Who Are You Really, Wanderer?
Pilgrimage and Rites of Way

Place works on the pilgrim ... that's what pilgrimage is for.
Rowan Williams

T he wanderer in me kicked off early. My first tentative pilgrimages began in my teens and covered a broad spread of cultural and quasi-spiritual quests. There was my first trip to Stratford-upon-Avon as a hopeful, wannabe actor, where I slept overnight on the steps of the Memorial Theatre. I travelled to see the Stones in the Park and also got swept up in the Grosvenor Square Riots. I even went along with a friend to be harangued by Billy Graham at one of his revivalist 'crusades'. And then one summer's morning, 'all un-looked for', something of The Other came into my life. I had walked, through the night, from Bournemouth railway station to Blandford Forum in Dorset. Ostensibly I was visiting an ailing aunt, but in reality I wanted to explore the literary/mythic landscape of Thomas Hardy, whom I'd recently come to admire. What I actually got was one of those mystical, peak experiences that seem to come to dispossessed, damaged or difficult young people in their teens. In my case it involved a life-changing moment, though it could actually have been an hour, when I found myself in the mist-wreathed, iron-age earthworks of Badbury Rings.

I was sixteen years old at the time and living on the edge of a precipice. I'd recently lost my father, was living alone in digs, and had failed most of my exams. That night I had walked, through varying degrees of darkness, up and out of Bournemouth and past Wimborne Minster. I was in a kind of teenage trance, when I found myself, footsore, hungry and exhausted, walking down a mile-long avenue of beech trees called Blandford Beeches. As the first faint light of dawn began to filter through the greenery, I left the road and headed for a distant hill that I sensed as much as saw off to my right. Through a wicket gate, I made my way over sheep-nibbled turf towards a circle of huge earth ramparts. Climbing up the first turf bank, I plonked myself down on the wet ground, and sat in silence, waiting for what seemed like hours. I was aware of the mist in the great ditch below me as it curled and shifted like so many waking snakes, burned off by the coming of the summer sun. And then something extraordinary happened.

Whether it was the fasting, or my state of exhausted sleeplessness – I hadn't eaten or slept for a couple of days at this point – I stumbled into the altered state that Native Americans enter when they undertake a vision quest[1]. As I sat, I noticed a small pink orchid, a banded snail making its way over the turf, and a blue-grey butterfly awaiting the heat of the day. I ran my hands over the grass and washed my face in morning dew. Then something made me turn, and I faced the rising sun. And suddenly, everything snapped into focus: the snail, the dew, the orchid and the butterfly; the great circling ramparts and the trees beyond the field. Everything was connected, and somehow trembling, and I was a part of it too. And so was everything I'd ever learned, or dreamed, or imagined. And running through it all, there was a kind of music, or rhythm. I could feel the beat of past and present, and the wheeling of the seasons. I could hear the deep, whale-like calling of the earth, and the wind through the blades of grass. And high above it all, the twittering of a skylark: a song so complete, so beautiful, that I was struck dumb like Kenneth Grahame's Rat and Mole when they meet the great god Pan at the gates of dawn.

Not long after that I shut down, in the way that teenagers do when faced with something they can't handle. And like the young knight Parsival and millions of other young people, I declined to ask the question at the core of my life. I shied away and concentrated on the external, on earning and spending, on getting by. However, the experience at Badbury Rings had planted a seed.

Later in life I found myself yearning for the countryside more and more. I settled into an annual pattern of walking holidays that were really times where I could be alone with myself, and reconnect with the landscape. This was how my pilgrimages evolved.

Every year I would choose a particular English county – Wiltshire or Shropshire, Suffolk or Herefordshire – in the unconscious hope of discovering a county where I felt I could settle or at least feel welcome. The idea was to walk randomly across each county, trusting to luck to show me the right places – and to find me a bed at night. I would buy an Ordnance

Survey map of the area, write to the local Tourist Information Offices and get a list of all the bed & breakfast establishments in the county. I'd give every one a number and then put little corresponding stickers on the map, and a phone number on the back. Every morning I would have my breakfast, and walk off without any plan or expectations. At lunchtime, I would head for the nearest public telephone box on the map (there were no mobile/cell phones back then). I would then look up the accommodation on the map, book myself a room, and head towards the B&B where I would have dinner. Nine times out of ten it worked out okay. I slept in the odd madhouse or gothic horror, and once slept in a barn because there was absolutely nothing available nearby. By degrees, I crisscrossed whole swathes of England, looking for somewhere, and learning more and more about the countryside that I had once turned my back on.

I surely had my burden, though I wasn't conscious of it. A pattern soon developed. I usually over-packed my rucksack and consequently struggled with it on the way: books, a tea-kettle and stove, far too many clothes. Then, naively, I would expect the map to be up-to-date, or at least correct. During the course of any sticky, irritable day, I could find myself chest deep in sunken lanes, surrounded by clumps of threatening stinging-nettles, or wandering round the edge of an overgrown field, trying to find a vanished footbridge across a fast-running river that was miles from the nearest crossing point. Needless to say this brought me face to face with a deep-seated rage that went back to the cradle. Many's the hot September day that found me lashing out wildly and viciously at the nettles, or swearing at the river in helpless impotence.

At such times the ghost of my father joined me. So I carried him too, along with my over-stuffed pack, struggling and cursing, and generally hating myself. One year, I started in Oxfordshire, by that mysterious chalk figure, the White Horse of Uffington. I walked for a week or more: past Wayland's Smithy, on to Barbury Castle, experiencing a particularly nasty little nettle-fight coming down off Hackpen Hill, via Avebury, past Silbury Hill and the West Kennet Long Barrow, through Savernake Forest, and then on, by way of Pewsey, and Stonehenge to Salisbury, where I sat engrossed, in a tea shop finishing a book called *England Their England* by A. G. MacDonnell[14].

This charming and occasionally very funny book had once been commended to me by my father, though it had been out of print back then, and I hadn't read it. I had absent-mindedly picked it up at a second-hand bookshop in Swindon as I passed through, and read it with great enjoyment on the road. There are, of course, no accidents in ritual, or on pilgrimage for that matter. The final scene of the book was set in Winchester where MacDonnell imagines a growing band of characters walking towards him in a kind of pageant of English history and culture. I read the last page, closed the book, and got the very next train to Winchester.

Arriving in Winchester, I remembered a story that my father, who was a Hampshire man, had once told me as a boy. He said there was a place called the Hospital of St Cross, a kind of almshouse, where for eight hundred years they had handed out a Wayfarer's Dole, a simple, and now largely symbolic, platter of bread and ale to anyone who asked.

Having sought directions, I walked from the railway station, down through the town and past the playing fields of Winchester College towards St Cross. My pack grew heavier as I walked over the water meadows by the River Itchen, and I rested in the shade of a broad, horse-chestnut tree, gazing into the waters as they trickled between the tree's exposed roots. I put my hand in my pocket and found an old penknife of my father's, which I had slipped into my pocket as I set out on my walk. I took it out and looked at it, and immediately I knew what I had to do. Slowly, deliberately, with all the solemnity of a true ritual, I unfolded the penknife, and cast it into the water.

I then made my way across the fields to the great stone pile of St Cross where, impressed by its isolated grandeur, I approached the gatehouse. I stood by the porter's lodge and waited respectfully, as I thought a wayfarer should. The porter came to the counter, cocked his head and looked at me. He waited a while and then, when I said nothing, inexplicably withdrew. And then I understood. They only gave out the Wayfarer's Dole to those who *asked*. After a while the porter returned.

"May I have my Wayfarer's Dole?" I said rather abruptly, repeating the rubric that had echoed in the gateway for eight hundred years. The porter smiled and brought out a wooden platter, which had a tiny square of sliced white bread and a small pottery beaker of ale upon it. Acutely conscious of the ritual moment, I ate and drank solemnly and gratefully, as if I were a starving pilgrim, as if my father were no longer with me.

Gradually, the unplanned climax of my pilgrimage unfolded. I looked back towards St Katherine's Hill, where the Scot, MacDonnell, had sat imagining English pilgrims walking towards him in the last scene of his book, and knew that I had turned some kind of a corner with regard to my father's persistent ghost. Lost in thought, I walked back across the water meadows, towards the cathedral. In its light-filled gothic interior I came across Jane Austen's grave, in a side aisle, with its overblown but charming inscription, in which her family fails to mention that she had written so much as a word, let alone soiled herself with novel-writing:

> "...The benevolence of her heart, the sweetness of her temper, and the extraordinary endowments of her mind obtained the regard of all who knew her and the warmest love of her intimate connections. Their grief is in proportion to their affection, they know their loss to be irreparable ..."

From Jane Austen's memorial I wandered along the north wall of the cathedral, entering what I later learned was the Epiphany Chapel. I sat on a modern chair, facing the altar, feeling nothing in particular beyond a calm induced by the Norman architecture and a deep, bone-sapping tiredness.

As I sat in the Epiphany Chapel, the cathedral choir began to rehearse the great Anglican rite of the sung Eucharist, the Evensong. By chance I was familiar with the piece, so I knew what was coming, or what might come, but I simply wasn't prepared for the pure, piercing voice of the boy treble who sang the solo introduction to Thomas Weelkes' *Nunc Dimittis*. "Lord lettest thou thy servant, depart in peace." The high, sweet yet solemn sound filled the cathedral and washed into the chapel, drowning me in memories, feelings and images. The air grew thick with grief and yearning.

As the Evensong unfolded and the sound of the choristers reverberated around the ancient building, my present frame of mind – my recent angry walks and resentment – collided with a memory of myself as a boy-chorister singing a solo, seeing my parents crying in the congregation.

As I mentioned in an earlier chapter, I had been born without a roof to my mouth. In the first year of my life, there had been hospitalisations, separations, and a new form of plastic surgery. The surgeon who operated on me had told my parents that I would probably never speak properly, and that I would, almost certainly, never be able to sing.

My mother, having already lost one baby, had taken this as a sign of her failure as a parent and retreated into a toxic shame that kept us apart for most of her life. My father, on the other hand, had taken it as a challenge and by the age of ten I was a soloist, auditioning for St Alban's Abbey choir. Now, in the Epiphany Chapel, I was strangely unable to look up. I saw my childhood laid out on the cold grey flagstones of the chapel floor. I saw how enmeshed my father and I had become. I saw his love and the drive to give me a voice. I saw the drink that clouded his judgment. I saw him lose his bearings, and cross a line. Finally I saw him hurting me.

And then I began to weep – from a place of raw, unravelling grief. Racked with sobs, I saw what had really taken place when I was a kid. How my father had lost the plot, and I had lost all innocence. But I also saw, despite all the shame and self-loathing, the rage and the isolation, that he was actually my only source of love – and that I still loved him. I started to grieve for him too, in a way that I had never been able to in my frozen adolescence, to grieve wholly and fully at last.

I remember my tears splashing on the flagstones, and my breath coming hard as I recalled my father's face. And I remember as I sat, pitched forward with my head on my arms, weeping uncontrollably in the Epiphany Chapel that a pair of cheap, grey, 'sensible' women's shoes came and sat beside me. A nun, I think, though I couldn't be sure, as I never looked up and we never exchanged a word. All the time I wept, and it seemed to go on for hours, I felt this woman beside me, neither prompting nor enquiring, simply present to my grief. By the time I stopped crying, the evensong was nearly over. As I sat there in silence, my head still down, she left as discreetly as she had arrived. I don't know who she was, or if she was even real, but I do know that she gave me a tremendous gift, and that I will always be grateful for it.

Coming away from Winchester I knew myself to be lighter, and in some indefinable way stronger. I had somehow managed to turn another miserable September ramble into a genuine pilgrimage. Not by heading for a religious site or signing up to serve a deity, but by offering up my burden, making it conscious and experiencing some of the backed-up, unfelt feelings I'd walked away from as a teenager. I still had a broad mass of issues to deal with, of course, but I had laid down something more than my rucksack on the flagstones of the Epiphany Chapel. I had owned some long-denied truths about my family, and by opening to the grime and gunk of my past, had lanced the boil of my twisted history. Perhaps most importantly, by acknowledging my love for my father, in spite of all he had done, I had allowed myself to love again at some point in the future.

~

There's something about a pilgrimage that can change you forever. It provides us with a ritual space in which to work out that which we need to attend to. Be it grief or anger, or suppressed desire, it will surely come up on the pilgrim's road. On pilgrimage, regardless of its impulse, we carry a burden of some kind that we hope to lay down. This can be at the end of our journey or at some point en route. It took me many journeys to realise this.

Sally Davies is a kind and generous woman, a cheerful level-headed mother and teaching assistant. On a recent walk with our spouses, along a path said to have inspired Wordsworth's "Lines Written a Few Miles Above Tintern Abbey", we fell to talking about ritual and the subject of pilgrimage. Knowing her to be an active and thoughtful Christian, I asked her for her sense of what lies at the core of pilgrimage. She considered my question for a while, then smiled her jolly, open-hearted smile. "Oh, I think it's about carrying something before you, don't you, of offering something to God?" I fell silent and thought about the journeys I'd made over the years; the trips, the hikes, the self-punishing route-marches. I saw that, with or without the involvement of a deity, this was exactly what I'd been trying to do. I'd been travelling to a point where I could lay something down; something heavy and dark and overwhelming. A few things began to make sense.

For our purposes then, a pilgrimage is a ritual journey, what writer and walker Robert MacFarlane neatly calls a 'rite of way'[15]. It can also be a metaphorical journey, a search, or a quest for something hidden and internal; something just out of sight, "just down the road and over the bridge"[16], as the Fisher King says to the eternal pilgrim Parsival when he reaches the land of dust and ashes we call the Waste Land. A pilgrim can be anyone from a penitent travelling to purge some perceived sin, to a bereaved friend quietly fulfilling a promise made at a deathbed; from an initiate seeking some insight or sign, to a secular tourist ticking off their bucket list.

Pilgrimage is as old as religion itself. Most religions attach spiritual significance to certain sites – usually the birth, death and transition places of its founders, avatars or saints. Other sacred sites commemorate the spiritual awakening, enlightenment or calling of the holy and their connection or return to the divine. Over time these places acquired added sanctity by the witnessing of miracles, or the housing of relics, precious objects, religious artefacts and memorabilia. Thus isolated caves, wells, mountains, islands, and similar places of withdrawal become attractive to the religious seeker who needs something more than a regular place of spiritual practice, who wants to forge a deeper connection to the source of his or her beliefs. What may have started out as a shaman's place of work, or a mystic's hideaway, becomes over time a place of communal healing or acknowledged connection. The accretions of time and the laying down of feelings, like nacre, form a glowing pearl that calls to us from a long way off. It speaks to that part of us that wants to see what's over the horizon, to the part of us that wants to go adventuring. It also touches us deeply, all the more so in our dislocated and rootless world, around our unmet desire for a sense of belonging; where the spiritual meets our primal need for place and a welcome, for a place in the heart.

There's a sweet and somewhat overlooked film called *The Way* made by Emilio Estevez, starring his father, Martin Sheen, which explores the internal struggles and emotional processes of a group of pilgrims walking the Camino toward the great Roman Catholic shrine of Santiago de Compostela in Galicia. Beginning near the Spanish-French border we follow Tom Avery, Sheen's character, as he wrestles with his grief for his son who died in a storm crossing the Pyrenees, while walking the Camino. Originally there to claim his son's remains, Avery decides to walk the ancient 'Way of St James' himself, and complete the journey for his dead son. On the way he meets three misfits who, like himself, are variously seeking meaning and a kind of absolution. By the time they arrive at their destination, Avery has taken a long deep look at his own character and his lack of faith, and learned to tolerate others. This is no Hollywood epic, but in a small yet generous way it shows us the conflicting feelings that come up when we begin to meet ourselves on a pilgrimage.

Pilgrimage appeals to the wanderer in us. Herman Hesse once said that we are either a wanderer or a sedentary burgher and that we can't be both. I'm not so sure. There comes a time when all sedentary folk feel the need to stretch their legs. And it's not just the Aboriginal peoples of Australia that go walkabout. The Hindu religion, for instance, has set up a system of *asramas* or stages of life that allow for people in their later years to go *sunyasin*, to literally give up their wealth and status, their responsibilities and even their relationships, and wander off in search of spiritual enlightenment, trusting to the generosity of the world. That seems pretty radical from a Western, secular point of view but it points to the millions of elderly baby-boomers we see, in retirement, visiting places of cultural importance, deepening their life experience and feeding on something long overlooked, or even shunned. I once wrote in a poem[17] that "time makes tourists of us all". Maybe it actually makes pilgrims of us.

So, what kind of pilgrimage can each of us make? Perhaps we can simply set out on a walk. We only need to begin. Lao Tse, the Taoist sage, said that a journey of a thousand miles begins with a single step. Once on our way, we can walk carrying a ritual object, like a seed or a stone, taking it from one place to another (our burdens need not all be heavy ones). We can walk for peace, go in search of the perfect cup of tea, or seek out the most beautiful view in the world. We can revisit the place where a loved one died, or go to the birthplace of a heroine or a role model. As we walk we can be sure that the world is working on us too, that the path before us is unfolding, and that we may be drawing ever closer to our deepest yearnings. Ritual journeys are not for everyone, but they do feed the wanderer in us. They can also bring us face to face with ourselves, and the world.

Chapter Six

Entering the Mysteries:
Rites of Passage for Modern Lives

Learning the language of initiation means finding in the inevitable struggles of our own lives ... the spiritual crises, the solitude, the despair through which every human being must pass in order to attain a responsible, genuine and creative life.

Mircea Eliade

It's a bright September day in Maine, and Juliet and I are spending some time out in the woods with W'abanaki ceremonialist, Tom Pesko. He's still a little unsure about us and I can see why – the last thing he needs is more white people helping themselves to his people's time-honoured ceremonies – but he's naturally polite and is taking his time to check us out. I suspect Tom may be a fine medicine teacher. He displays all the attributes of the wounded healer and has a grief about him that makes me feel at home, particularly when he talks about the big shiny eco-homes his community built at the edge of the village, and the trees they chopped down to make way for them. You can feel the pain in him as he swims against the tide of history and cultural decline. It was the loss of the trees that really hurt.

Tom is showing us the ritual ground he uses for the ceremonies he performs – an elegantly constructed natural space of two connected circles in the woods with fire pits, ceremonial tipi and sweat lodge. It's holy ground.

Tom performs sweat lodges for his community, but his work has taken a turn since he returned from his travels. Back home amongst what he calls "the sickness" – the toxic Western 'disease' of consumerism, addiction and celebrity culture that erodes tribal ways – he began to see that he needed to provide ways for the vulnerable young people of his nation to reclaim their culture and their pride. He started quietly patching together his rituals, herb lore and teaching into a highly effective rite of passage. He wouldn't call it that, of course; he's neither an anthropologist nor a middle-class new-ager, but he has been doing what elders have done across the millennia. Amidst the stresses and difficulties of life, he has found a way to initiate the young people of his threatened culture into responsible adulthood.

Despite his disillusionment and his sense of isolation, Tom is almost single-handedly working to help the young men of his community whose lives are blighted for lack of mentors and proper initiations. Between the alcohol, the petty crime and the crack, he's facing an uphill struggle.

As we walk around we meet three young lads. The first is lost in a world of his own: flat, vague and unable to connect. I would have thought he was stoned but Tom says not. He looks so blank because he's been snorting lighter fluid since he was twelve and he's permanently strung out. However, he's nosing around the ritual ground, which is a good sign. He's curious and might 'come in'. As he leaves, we see the white flash of a deer's rump, off to the right, as it bobs away through the undergrowth. Tom looks at us sideways.

Further down the track another lad appears. He is more open. He makes an effort, mumbles the odd question and tries to stand still. Tom introduces us and the lad struggles to maintain contact. He makes a few jerky observations but then abruptly leaves with a clumsy wave of a hand. "He's a good kid – about ready. I think I can help him. He wants to come along to help me do ceremony." He falls silent as an unseen deer crashes away from us.

We walk on in silence. Ahead of us we see a third young man on a bicycle, who waves and stops to say hello. He is very different, a friendly young American, outgoing and full of clear-eyed enthusiasm. He exchanges pleasantries with Tom, then beams a cheerful farewell to us, pops his earphones back in, and heads off on his bike. Tom explains that he was once as far down the line as the other guys. He'd got into drugs and was about to flunk out of school, when he'd become curious about Tom's work and started to hang around. After his first ceremony he went straight home, cleared out his dope and took down his Bob Marley poster, gave it to his mom and asked her to burn it. He went back to school, turned his grades around, and was now studying law with a view to helping the community in their ongoing battles with the State and its various environmental agencies.

I half expect a deer to make itself heard, but there is nothing but the gentle soughing of the wind in the pines above us. Tom is cautiously explaining how he is working to put something back into his community, trying to initiate kids back into their own traditions as a way of dealing with the modern world's complexities. We'd seen both the 'before' and the 'after' and his story was compelling. These young lads desperately need some grounding, not to mention the presence of a benign, dependable male in their lives. If they were to claw their way back to any kind of a life, Tom is probably their best, if not their only hope.

As we exchanged experiences, I began to see Tom as a genuine warrior-shaman, fighting for a people who had suffered centuries of dispossession and cultural collapse. His tragedy is that, even as we in the West are finally getting the message about the need for appropriate initiations for youth, in the villages and reservations of Native America, many people seem to be turning away from the old, cohesive structures that could create meaningful rites of passage. They are abandoning their kids to self-initiation and the dance with death. Tom was out there on his own.

As we stood there, it was as if Tom was making up his mind about us. We seemed genuine enough I'm sure, but a lifetime of tribal disappointments was working against us. We were about to make our farewells and return to Albion Pond when we, all three of us, went very still. About a hundred yards down the path that led into the woods, first one, and then a second, and then a third white-tailed deer stepped out on the path, the last one pausing to look at us before calmly moving off into the woods. Tom looked after the deer and then back at us. "Come back to our house," he said at last, smiling. "My wife has made soup and bread. We can talk."

~

Initiation is often seen as a primitive induction into manhood for indigenous youth. That's wrong. Firstly, initiation is not confined to the male gender; secondly, it is far from primitive; and thirdly, initiation in those cultures that still employ it is not confined to any one period of life. In such cultures, initiations are seen as necessary throughout life and are thought of as gateways to the next stage of an individual's development. In fact, initiations give us the psychological and emotional tools to deal with what life has in store for us. As Malidoma Somé has said, such rituals initiate us into the next round of trouble.

Unfortunately, we in the West have largely failed to address our lack of initiation and our very human need for rites of passage. Two World Wars and the Industrial Revolution have swept away our sacred technologies and left nothing in their place. They have created a situation in which adults remain habitually unsure of themselves, until such time as life randomly initiates them through acts of war, childbirth, sickness and aging.

As Michael Meade, a true expert on initiation, says, "Ancient peoples invented rites of passage in part to break the spell of childhood and move the initiate from the mother's lap to the lap of the world. To this day, a person must dismantle the spell of childhood or fail to find their place in life."[18]

Today, too many of our adults remain spellbound. Still enmeshed in the spells of childhood, they can be spotted in their infantilised clothing, their childish behaviour, and in their unending need to pit themselves against their parents, or authority. This becomes even more alarming when we look at our leaders, who tend to be petulant, grandiose, visibly self-doubting, and altogether too enamoured of war. It was partly because of this absence of maturity in the general Western population that the exploration of ritual and initiation became a key plank of the work of Robert Bly and others in the late eighties. Bly's long, hard look at what he called the Naïve Male opened up a rich seam.

Since then there has been a gradual growth of interest in rites of passage, to the point where they are increasingly seen as a good thing. Following on from Arnold Van Gennep and Victor Turner's groundbreaking work on the stages of initiatory rituals, Joseph Campbell's influential *The Hero's Journey*[19] informed and inspired all manner of developments and digressions, from *Star Wars* and books on three-act movie structure, through to overtly religious rites of passage and heavily programmed boot camps for men and troubled youth. In amongst all this excitement, it is sometimes hard to keep sight of the simple, elegant ritual that is a rite of passage.

The essential feature of any rite of passage is that it involves the three stages originally observed by Van Gennep, those of *Pre-liminaire, Liminaire* and *Post-liminaire* which Joseph Campbell re-dubbed *Separation, Ordeal* and *Return*, and which I prefer to think of as *Separation, Transition* and *Incorporation*. Whatever we call them, the three-fold natural divisions of a beginning, a middle and an end are never more powerful than in a rite of passage.

The purpose of the *Separation* phase is to remove the initiate from the world of daily doing, and pitch them into the 'otherworld' of liminality, symbol and being. Historically, separations were usually physical. At the first sign of sexual interest, for instance, youngsters would be taken off to the tribe's initiation hut where they lost their identity and joined a peer group of initiates for the duration of the rite. The initiate was cut off from the life they knew, regardless of age or gender. Other separations involved journeys out into nature or more figurative descents into underground initiation chambers. Whatever the geographical or symbolic degree of separation, it achieved a psychological detachment from such things as home, mother, belonging, and safety. The initiate crossed a *limen*, a threshold, and entered ritual space.

The *Transitional* phase is the core of any rite of passage. Having created a shift in the initiate's consciousness, the process then further alters his/her state. In my experience this has included drumming, time alone in nature, enforced silence, and the recitation of stories. Drumming is often a key part of any ritual and the communal beating of drums can have a profound effect on any group. It gets you into your body and turns a gathering of individuals into a bonded 'band' that increasingly touches something deeper as it plays together. If done at the shamanic beat of 120 beats per minute, a drum can alter your state very quickly.

There's been a lot of ink spilt over the use of hallucinogenic drugs in indigenous ceremony, with talk of mushrooms, acid and latterly *ayahuasca*, but there's very little need to use drugs in any modern day initiation. Between the drumming and the increased geographical shift of modern initiations (many people cross continents to experience these rites), there's already a considerable alteration of state by the time a person 'lands' in the *Transitional* stage.

The purpose of the *Transitional* stage of any modern rite of passage is to create a change in the initiate, a radical shift in their self-perception and/ or their map of the world that leaves them internally, and often externally, different. This can culminate in a declaration, a sudden understanding, or a decisive ritual action. It usually involves a challenge to their view of themselves and as such can be a real test of character and resolve. It need not necessarily be a full-on ordeal.

Campbell's idea of *Ordeal* has a powerful romantic charge to it, but has led many literalists down some ugly, and in some cases downright abusive, paths. There's the horrible story of a community of fathers berating and shaming their teenage sons "because that's what the world is like". Actually it merely implants a memory of being shunned to add to their poor kids' woes. So, while there *is* a definite element of testing in any decent rite of passage, there is also something about exchange here, and gift, and fundamentally, empowerment.

Some of the *Transitional* challenges I have seen have involved descents into grief for men who were strangers to their feelings, nights spent alone in the wilds, and confrontations with representations of bullies or abusers, each and every one suitably 'safe' within the context of a ritual challenge. And, of course, it's not all about noisily overcoming fears or past oppressions. Some transitions I've seen were so quiet that you might have missed them entirely. These have included tender awakenings to intimacy, gentle resolutions of long-distressing enmities, silent atonements, and profound realisations around the onset and acceptance of aging.

Having experienced the *Transitional* stage, people invariably need space and time for reflection. This is a crucial part of any rite of passage that can easily be overlooked. In our "okay-what's-next" world we have a habit of moving on when, in reality, we need to sink into our experience and assimilate. This is why I like the word *Incorporation* rather than Campbell's simpler *Return*. *Incorporation* speaks to a kind of absorption – a taking into the *corpus*, the body – an essential integration of learning or understanding about the shift in identity or status that has occurred.

There is, of course, an aspect of return in the *Incorporation* stage, which implies a return to normality as much as to a locale or home. In indigenous cultures this provides grounds for a welcoming feast, often involving the entire community. Such celebrations serve to parade the visible changes embodied in the initiates, and to put food in their bellies. This, like fish and chips after a football match or movie, serves to reconnect them to the known and the familiar. Such grounding prevents the returnees from remaining stuck in potentially dangerous liminal spaces. In modern rites of passage *Incorporation* is rightly given a great deal of attention. Group discussions, communal meals and a certain amount of physical activity, particularly cleaning up, all serve to prepare people for re-entry into their normal lives.

~

My own involvement in rites of passage began when I joined the Everyman/ Wild Dance Rites of Passage programme, which ran for a decade at Cae Mabon, in Snowdonia. I worked as an assistant and later as a co-leader of these retreats, which were led, in my time, by Ron Pyatt, a psychotherapist, painter and gifted ritualist[20].

The programme grew out of the growing interest in rites of passage in the eighties. Founded by Eric Maddern, a storyteller, Alex Wildwood, a Quaker and Justin Kendrick, a social anthropologist, it followed the classic template of all rites of passage. It did however evolve to incorporate new discoveries and learnings, not the least of which were the understandings that access to nature needed to be an integral part of any modern rite, and that the shadow, the often darker but always hidden side of human nature, needed to be aired if modern-day initiates were to get any benefit from such a process.

An ability to hold and contain negative behaviours, or allow the display of hidden talents, is essential if ritual is to thrive. The rageful woman, beside herself at the grief shrine, the man making some unexpected object of beauty, or the aggrieved comic calling out, "Where's my fifty bucks," at the graveside, are all expressing their shadow in a healthy ritual way. This is where the modern world has failed us. As we have become ever more sophisticated we have banished the wild and unpredictable from our ritual lives, turning Dionysian descent and shadowy cleansing into polite, controlled, and consequently lifeless, ceremonial. The Rites of Passage programme found a way back to something dark and edgy, and so created a container that was genuinely challenging, cleansing and invigorating.

The Rites of Passage programme was thus both a potent evolution of an ancient practice and an initiatory retreat that abided by the principles of a traditional rite of passage. At the same time it opened up the frame for people of any age, usually men in those days, who were facing a transition in their lives or wanted to work on something that was blocking them. It catered for the modern predicament.

By the time I joined, the form was tried and tested. Over five days, participants travelled through the classic stages: bonding as 'instant communities'; experiencing time alone in nature; deepening their understanding of themselves and their shadow; developing trust and pooling their wisdom to create initiations of authenticity, profound meaning, and occasional magic, under the quiet, watchful eye of Ron Pyatt.

Ron had the classic artist-shaman's instinctive grasp of ritual, knowing when to call the shots and when to allow the liminal magic of the moment to emerge. I learned by osmosis and watched like a hawk as Ron, cautiously and with great humility, tailored rite after rite, to the point where they were exactly what the initiate needed in their life. His work had a care and a precision that meant that his rituals landed, exactly, time after time.[21] In my ritualising, I had discovered that I needed rigour and impeccability. Ron Pyatt had both qualities; as much as any indigenous shaman or medicine teacher I ever worked with.

One of the important tenets of the Rites of Passage programme was that anyone leading such a process had to have been through their own initiation. I was no exception and my rite of passage unfolded one warm May afternoon, when Ron realised that I was 'cooked', that is emotionally engaged and 'ripe' to undergo my tailor-made rite of passage. Having been formally offered and accepted my ritual, I was ritually blindfolded and sent off to a hut to await my fate, and waited for hours. While I was away the group discussed my situation and came to a precise formulation fairly quickly. It was decided that I had become too closely identified with my painful past; that I was ready to move on but locked into my victim status, and somehow stuck, ploughing the same old furrow of wounded manhood. The plan was to give me a ritual that moved me on, beyond victimhood, and encouraged me to fulfill my potential. What greeted me as I was led out of my hut and had my blindfold removed was a strange reconfiguration of the site. On a field in front of me, a man was ploughing a furrow repeatedly. I was then taken to a perfectly circular pool that had appeared in the yard (the creation of this beautiful pool had taken hours of digging into the solid slate of the hillside!). Here I was asked to take off my clothes and sit in the pool, which was filled with warm mud, and to mark, with mud, all the places on my body where I had been hurt or abused or shamed. It was deeply moving and seemed to take forever as I dabbed at my body. As I repeated my story once more, my shame was real enough, but it wasn't overwhelming and I began to feel that I was taking up people's time. At which point Ron and a friend appeared in front of me. Smiling broadly, they splashed me with finger-fulls of mud. I needed no prompting. I splashed them back and we were suddenly enjoying a full-on mud fight, laughing like six-year-olds.

This good-humoured aspect of the work was integral to Ron Pyatt's method. Like Shakespeare, who always ended the cathartic ritual of a tragedy with a lighthearted jig, Ron was always keen that we found a way to end on a point of celebration, with either a return to the 'village' that the community represented or through a kind of internal 'welcome back to reality', which he achieved through a deft mixture of openhearted clowning and straightforward old-style celebration.

In my case, when the laughter subsided and I had washed in the stream, I was taken to a hut, which had been beautifully decorated in rich greenery and bracken. I was laid down on a mattress, and left alone to listen to the birdsong and relax in the sunshine that poured in through the windows. As I listened to the sounds of the others chatting outside and enjoying the mud pool, I suddenly realised that life was really very beautiful and that my past really was behind me. It was time for me to be someone else.

~

Working up in Snowdonia, I came to see that rites of passage were more than just handy mechanisms for personal change. They were vital tools for social and communal cohesion. They offered a way for all age groups, classes, and castes to experience and internalise major life-changes in competence, status and self-perception. Be it with troubled youth, or elders, rites of passage, by piloting change and settling people in their altered circumstances, can help people to fit more harmoniously in their communities. This is never more necessary than in the return of soldiers from the hellish underworld of war.

As we have become ever more sophisticated war-makers, we have become less and less adept at returning service men and women to their homes and families. It's ironic, but we ritualise the entry of countless people into our armed forces. We cut their hair, change their identity, and change them radically from the youngsters who turn up at boot camps around the world. Then, after numerous tours of duty in places where death and horror are commonplace, they are abruptly put on a plane, given a paycheck, and dumped back on the streets of the town they joined the military to leave. It is no surprise that they become angry, anti-social individuals; they are still stuck in the dark liminal spaces of their stressful experience.

On one particular Rites of Passage retreat, we found ourselves addressing this increasingly pressing problem directly, and in the process found a ritual solution for returning soldiers. One of the participants was a retired NCO of twenty-two years' service, who had been sent to us by his girlfriend who was finding it hard to cope with his inability to settle back into society after leaving the army. His ritual became clear as we discussed his circumstances: a decorated soldier who was full of mixed feelings about his past and all the things he had seen and done.

Coming out of the hut where he had been sent to await his ritual, our warrior was confronted by a circle of men. One of us recounted the tale of Cuchullain, the Irish hero, whose blind, raging battle-lust was so great that the women of the village bared their breasts to stop him as he returned home. The women led him to three great vats of water, and plunged him into each one. The first he burst asunder with his rage, the second he steamed off in his fury, but in the third vat he stopped, and he wept, at which point he was allowed back into the village.

Once the story was told we asked our warrior to create a cairn of pieces of slate at a point half way up the track by the stream. Each piece of slate was to represent some cause of anger, or shame, or grief. We other men formed a silent guard of honour at intervals along the track, to witness his ritual.

What we hadn't realised was that we really were dealing with a warrior. Where we had imagined small handfuls of rock he found huge shards of slate. Carrying them up and down the hill like some mythic hero, he built a huge cairn of stone whose ugliness increased with every exhausting addition and every crashing arrival. We stood in awed respect as his cairn grew by the hour – and it took hours. Finally, exhausted, he stopped. We led him down to the stream, which we had dammed with stones to create a pool, and dunked him in the cold mountain water – once, twice, three times. He later said that this was the most 'scary' part of the ritual for him. Finally he was led back down the track to the barn where he was formally welcomed back to the village, sat on a throne and asked "What are you going to serve now?"

Years later our warrior is an experienced tracker and therapist who has gained an MSc and created his own pathfinder school using nature to heal and help individuals and communities.

~

In a very real sense this form got as close as any work I have ever seen to what the Greeks used to call The Mysteries – the Eleusinian Mysteries. These were the ancient, secret, initiatory rituals held in celebration of the earth goddesses Demeter and Persephone in which participants experienced "descent", "loss" and "ascent" as a way of assuring a better life. If we take away the religious precept we are left with a remarkable parallel to the rites of passage. Some have said that The Mysteries were dependent on psychedelic substances. My experience with both the shamans, and now on the rites of passage, was there is no need for drugs. The magic was and is in the ritual.

Crucially, what the Rites of Passage programme had achieved was to set up a non-religious form that welcomed any belief system while operating within secular bounds. This allowed for an extraordinary phenomenon, which seemed to bring both a kind of 'magic' to the rites of passage and, to me at least, a deeper understanding of the connectivity of all things. Ron would have called this a sense of correctness, of impeccability, a kind of collective knowledge. "It was about accessing what was right," he would say. "If it didn't come you just waited." From where I sat watching him, on days when the rituals flowed and people were served in the most creative and caring of ways, I saw someone akin to the sages of China: increasingly wise, patient and infinitely accepting. And behind him, if not the absolute, all embracing Tao of Chinese philosophy, a 'field' of universal knowing that linked and informed both the participants and the team – a field that induced life-changing peak experiences.

Ron would never have countenanced any such speculation, of course. For him it was essential to maintain a non-philosophical line. It would always be about the individual and their personal changes. And he was right. In our modern world, the essential core of the Rites of Passage programme was its ability to meet and deal with the human shadow. This reminded me of a hard but essential truth that I had picked up in the recovery community. You can't *really* get spiritual until you've cleaned house, which means that you have to deal with your past, whatever it holds, before you can even hope to step onto any genuine spiritual path. As the Sunday-paper parade of addicted gurus, disgraced politicians and defrocked priests shows us, our dark, shadow behaviours and our family histories are deeply embedded within us. If we don't deal with them they will come back to haunt us. It was the days of shadowy descent and personal work that allowed for the remarkably pure, transcendent moments and peak experiences of the rites of passage performed up at Cae Mabon. Together they made for a true, modern Mystery.

Chapter Seven

Wounded Doves and Broken Vines:
Rituals of Separation, Parting and Closure

A ritual wouldn't be a ritual if you didn't feel like
you'd been put through the wringer, would it?
James Burke

I used to hate holidays, or vacations as they call them in America. My dysfunctional background had bred a deep anxiety in me, fed by weeks of childhood holiday misery, and fuelled by the shame of my parents' drinking and incessant public rowing in hotels and theatres. So there's a delightful irony that I should now be spending my summers in *Vacationland*, which is what the State of Maine calls itself, at least on its number plates. Juliet has taught me to love holidays. I still have my edgy moments, but the idea of a few weeks off, pottering or writing in the mornings and loafing in the afternoons, no longer fills me with dread. This morning, as I sit here looking out at the clouds reflected in the placid waters of Albion Pond, I can see the many ways that I have changed. There is no one single point at which one qualifies or graduates as a ritualist. I had imagined that there would be a great initiatory moment when I would feel the proverbial poke from a sharp stick, but I had experienced so many initiations in my life, and the ongoing process was so mysterious that I simply woke up one clear morning with the understanding that I had changed at a cellular level. What had been a dark and rocky road had become a well-worn path, and what had been a threatening, even treacherous environment had become a living, vibrant, and responsive world. Studying under my teachers, gradually reconnecting with people, and rediscovering my core connection with nature, I had simply *become* a ritualist.

It started with people asking me to help them bury their cats or dogs, to help them honour both their animals' passing and the loving connections they had felt with their pets. Then came requests to conduct the weddings and funerals of friends and colleagues, and the odd ritual to celebrate a significant birthday or anniversary. At one point I considered going professional and setting up as a celebrant. As time went by, however, something else happened that shifted my focus. People started coming to me with their personal problems, which they hoped might be 'fixed' or at least addressed with a ritual: to lift a depression perhaps, or to begin a project; to change some behaviour, or to cope with some external change forced upon them by circumstance. I started doing small, individual, more 'radical' rituals to help them realign their lives or address a knotty problem. I never advertised myself or hung up my shingle, as an American might put it. I simply made no secret of what I did and said yes to most requests in the belief that our common wisdom would find a way. Gradually the rituals I was asked to perform became more and more complex.

This was because they sought to address the lacks and the gaps in the ritual lives of our increasingly complex society. Some of the most pressing and necessary rituals I have been asked to perform have been rituals of separation. Whilst we still have the wedding, with its powerful bonding symbol of the wedding ring, we have no equivalent ritual for those who want to separate or have actually parted. If we are lucky we can 'kiss and part', but the reality is, more often than not, that one spouse wants a separation less than the instigator and, despite all protestations to the contrary, remains deeply attached. Over time this enmeshment, this sense of unfinished business and attachment, can cause a suppurating wound that spills its bitterness over any potential future relationship. It leaves the person left behind isolated, often depressed and full of regret. The difficulty is that the authorities that married them created their 'entry rituals' into the institution of marriage in the dim and distant past when no one thought of people *exiting* such an arrangement, except through the attrition of widowhood. The tragedy is that today, these same authorities feel unable to provide the ritual healing, or in more extreme cases the ritual cauterization, necessary to bring closure to a failed relationship that was entered into with full, communal ceremony, and is visibly calling for a ritual ending.

~

Joe had been living with a partner for some years. He had loved her and dreamed of raising a family with her. As far as he was concerned, she was perfect for him and, truth to tell, he had changed and grown considerably under her influence. He was therefore mortified when she finished the relationship. She balked (at least in his eyes) at the emotional work that a long-term relationship would have demanded and abruptly headed off to Canada, to continue her personal cycle of broken relationships and crashed romances.

Joe came to me some years later. He had tried to form new relationships, had at least dated other women, but he was plagued by the memory of his one great love. No one else came up to his estimation of her in either looks or intelligence. "I can't get her out of my mind," he said. "Even though I know it's over and she'll never come back. I need one of those separation rituals you were talking about."

We agreed to go to a place of his choosing in the countryside and I gave him a short list of things to acquire before he met me again. He turned up at the appointed hour before dawn and we travelled down empty roads to the country in time for the half-light to greet us.

His chosen site was a forlorn, empty meadow, with scrub behind us and a ridge ahead, which had straggly old crab-apples and hawthorns dotted along it. As the light grew we set up the ritual space by laying out his 'props'. Then, in line with his spiritual beliefs which had grown out of his fascination with Celtic shamanism and 'the old ways' as he called them, we invoked the ancestors and the spirits of place. First, I spoke to the four cardinal directions, then to the spirits of all we could see around us. I imagined those who had lived on the land over the generations and made it what it was that day. Thus spirits of oak and hawthorn, crab-apple and thistle were invoked alongside the ancestral spirits of shepherd and woodsman, dairymaid and wise-woman, priest and warrior. This induced a visible relaxation in Joe, that sense of homecoming which made the place his as much as anyone's for the duration of his ritual.

He dug a hole and we knelt at either side of it, opposite each other. I asked him for the old sheet that they had once used on their bed when they lived together and checked that he had made a couple of dozen inch-deep incisions along one hem. He had. I then tore the sheet in half lengthways and retained a half, giving him the other. The sound of the tearing sheet sounded unnaturally loud in this strangely quiet dawn.

Nothing invokes a sense of separation, or a parting of the ways, so much as the tearing of a length of cloth. I'm not sure whether it's the rending sound or the slow destruction of something once valued and useful, but the visceral rip of the material, and the person's absolute control of the parting

– now fast, now unbearably slow, now hurried, now full of inexorable tension – brings on a sense of finality like nothing else, nothing except the reverberating silence *after* the tearing.

When asked, Joe recited a prepared list of all the things he had seen as good in their relationship: their friendship, their shared spirituality, their love of music. At the recitation of each and every good thing, I took up the sheet and tore it. As the strips came free I threw them into the hole Joe had dug. By the time he had finished he was weeping. I got him to dry his eyes on the sheet that he was holding.

Next I asked him to take up the other half of the sheet and name all that had been bad in the relationship: the betrayal, the abandonment, and the running away from a good thing. This time Joe tore the sheet at every statement, his anger rising with the expression of each disappointment and petty deception, his ripping action more fierce with every tear. Even as he tried to 'understand' his ex, her selfish behaviours became all the more apparent and he tore at the cloth with increasing energy. Finally, he got down to his buried feelings of hurt and anger, which he bellowed into the hole in the ground. With the cloth now shredded and practically filling the hole, I asked him to take up the other two objects that I had asked him to bring, which represented their relationship: a pair of hand-painted mugs with their names on, which she had bought but left behind. He took the mug with her name on it and tearfully placed it in the hole on the shredded cloth. He then threw the other mug in the hole with all his might, smashing both. Having 'made the break' he read out a statement, which I had asked him to write: a statement of his love, his hurt and his intention to both 'get over it' and move forward into more appropriate and loving relationships. Having finished, he paused, and then added an impromptu, powerfully affirmative statement about his desire for children and his belief that he would eventually find the right woman. Finally we closed the hole with soil, tamped it down, turned to face the rising sun with its symbolic new beginning, and Joe called on his ancestors and the spirits of place to witness what he had done.

~

On another occasion, I worked with a couple, Annie and Ted, who had decided that they wanted to separate. In fact it was Ted who wanted to move on, while Annie was ambivalent about parting, and was 'letting him go' in what felt like a rather generous if one-sided arrangement. They turned up on the day with two friends to serve as witnesses. They brought their representative objects, both of which happened to be wooden, and a length of coloured cloth that had once meant a lot to them and seemingly still did to Annie. As we proceeded I became aware of a kind of politeness in the proceedings that I found quite distasteful. Annie was subdued as she tentatively tore up her half of the cloth, compliantly naming what she had enjoyed and resented in their time together, while Ted was being conciliatory but clearly just going through the motions. At one point he said that he was going to miss her hugs and affection, and even said that he would like to finish the ritual with a hug. Annie smiled but I thought I could detect a frisson of irritation, the kind of frisson that in another culture would have her hitting him!

I followed an intuition and suggested that we burn the objects in the hole rather that bury them as previously agreed and tore some pages from my notebook to get the fire going. I then asked them each to add their wooden objects and we stood back and watched as the flames took hold. I then asked Ted to take a step towards the fire and read his statement. It sounded oddly cruel, for all its concerns about freedom and 'having tried to make things work'. One of the witnesses coughed uncomfortably. I was watching Annie at this point, half expecting her to cry but she seemed quite composed. All I could see was that her throat was mottled red and that she seemed to have stopped breathing. I asked Ted to put his statement into the fire, which he did, and stepped back from the fire. Annie stepped forward.

As she was about to speak, I followed an intuition and stepped forward. I took her statement from her, cast it into the fire and said, "Say what you need to say, Annie. Just speak from your heart."

"I can't," she said.

"Why not?"

"I'm so…" she ground to a halt.

"Upset?" I offered, happy to be wrong.

"No, angry. And I always end up crying when I'm angry. It's so humiliating. I really, really don't want to cry."

I turned to Ted and asked him whether he was prepared, as a parting gift, to listen to Annie's anger. Could he stand before her, and not shut her down or shame her but simply hear her anger? He blanched at this but said that he would.

I thanked him and reminded him to keep breathing throughout, and gently said that all would be well.

I then got our two patient witnesses to stand either side of Annie and to link arms with her, facing backwards as she faced forwards, ensuring that she was safely held and supported by their physical presence. I then said, "You are perfectly safe, Annie. This is exactly the right place and time to say what you have to say." I was about to give her some more encouraging advice but she cut me off.

"You *bastard*!" It came like a train out of a tunnel at a hundred miles an hour. Ted looked like he had been whacked on the nose. I took a step towards him and reminded him to keep breathing. He acknowledged this with a nod and bravely turned back to face Annie's fury. She told him to stick his hug, his patronising ways, and his little-boy whining, and generally kept on expressing herself, very powerfully, until she ran out of steam. Ted, subdued and abashed, looked down at the burning symbols of his relationship as the flames began to gutter.

"I'm sorry, Annie," he said. "I'm really sorry." There was a pause, while he waited for her forgiveness but it wasn't forthcoming, so he looked up and then looked away. Annie shook herself free of her support and faced him over the fire.

"I deserve better," she said, "and I'm going to have a fantastic life."

And so Ted got to end the relationship and move on. However, equally importantly, Annie got to separate too. Rather than go inwards, become depressed and self-blaming in her abandonment, she was able to express her sense of betrayal and outrage and, crucially, maintain her self-respect.

Some people, including celebrants, seek to make separation rituals an affirmative and loving experience. "It should be about moving on positively and lovingly into the next phase of life," says one experienced celebrant. All well and good, but let us not forget the purpose of the ritual. We want a separation, and in any separation, something has to die. This will, almost inevitably, result in grief and pain. There will also, probably, be a degree of imbalance, with one partner seeking the separation more or less than the other. While it is good to entertain the hope that both partners will ultimately embrace change and step forward positively into the next stage of their separate lives, it is naïve to imagine that this will always be the case. Often one partner harbours hurts too deep to name, and too raw to acknowledge at the time, even to themselves. In such cases a separation ritual can serve to flush out the feelings, and allow for a healthy, if momentarily painful, cauterisation, and create in both partners a sense of balance. To force anyone into a 'positive' experience, when deep inside they are hurting, is at best disrespectful and at worst potentially dangerous.

Likewise, some celebrants say that there should be no anger or resentment in separation rituals. I'm not so sure that I agree. A feeling is a feeling is a feeling. If it is appropriate to the ritual, it will surely come up and we stifle feelings at our peril. As long as the person expressing their feelings has someone to 'spot' for them, like any gymnast or weightlifter, to ensure that they are safe and that they don't hurt themselves or others, all will ultimately be well. In these circumstances it is the task of the person 'receiving' the anger to remain present, keep breathing, and allow the other's feelings to be expressed appropriately, in the belief that they are clearing toxic feelings that would otherwise poison them. Anger, of course, can also be a cover for a deeper grief, which the ritual, if it is properly held, will safely expose and process, allowing a greater degree of healing than if it is suppressed. Anger and grief are inextricably linked: how many fights and arguments have we seen at funerals!

So, while it is often appropriate to set a positive intention for a separation ritual, we need to allow whatever feelings that arise to be expressed openly. This allows for everyone present to witness and accept the emotional reality of the separation, and for the person expressing the feelings to be honoured in them too. Likewise in such rituals it is important that everyone is allowed to express their feelings fully without being soothed or comforted out of them. Our friends are always alive to our pain and some of them would rather we didn't express our hurt or rawness. Some, like Ted, may even want to hug us or soothe us in a 'there-there-don't-cry' kind of way. This is far from helpful and is usually as much about their own discomfort around deep feelings as an attempt to help the person they are intent on 'comforting'. It certainly doesn't serve the ritual and, in the long term, it doesn't serve anyone in it.

Chapter Eight

Coming Back In:
Deep Rituals of Alignment and Healing

Mastery is achieved by letting things take their natural course.
Forcing things achieves nothing.
Lao Tzu - Tao Te Ching

Unless the relationship between the living and the dead is in balance,
chaos ensues.
Malidoma Patrice Somé

T he various nature-based creeds and philosophies of the world speak of a kind of oneness in which everything is flowing together in a fundamental harmony of the human and the non-human, the material and the spiritual. This active confluence of the natural, invisible and human worlds is no longer understood in the largely secular West, while it's a given in other cultures where simple unforced alignment with this flow is obvious, desirable and normal. In this context, being out of kilter with, or going wilfully against, the recognised tide of life, calls for careful rituals to get one back into alignment and sympathy.

When I set out on the ritual path, I couldn't quite understand why I might need to realign myself with anything, let alone some invisible flow of life. Firstly, as a typical Westerner, I was wedded to the cult of the individual and my sense of self, and secondly, I had no real attachment to anything, let alone the earth, or spirits. It wasn't until I had travelled a little and seen that other cultures don't raise the individual above the community (or nature, God or The Invisibles) that I understood that one could be out of whack with that which surrounds us.

Later, when I was studying Malidoma Somé's work on radical rituals, which I'd always thought of as rituals of *healing*, I came to realise that what he was actually describing was a body of ritual that sought to balance the needs of the living with the desires and imperatives of The Other – in his case the dead, the ancestors. This was a lot for me to take in, and it wasn't until I re-visited the Tao Te Ching's concept of *Wu Wei*, the Watercourse Way, that our spiritual, mental and physical health depends on us going with the greater flow of life, that I appreciated the full picture.

Whether it be with our communities or the environment, with spirits or the ancestors, we've all experienced times when we've found ourselves out of balance, exiled from what a Christian might call a state of grace. At such times we can become deeply unhappy. We feel lost and cut off. At such times a ritual of alignment can provide a lifeline. It can bring us back in.

~

Becky was in her mid-thirties, slim, red-haired and determined to be chirpy. She came to me via a friend who thought that a ritual might help her to solve a particular issue that had been plaguing her for some years. We met and talked things through and it quickly became apparent that she was suffering from a problem that has become all too common in our modern society. Some decade or more before she had had an abortion, without her boyfriend's knowledge. She had later married him and had a son whom they both adored. She felt she couldn't tell her volatile (and on one occasion, violent) husband about the abortion but she was increasingly prey to nightmares and 'flashbacks' of her abortion experience and fantasies about her aborted daughter; she was adamant that the foetus had been female. We agreed that I would provide a ritual for her and that we would address her problem together.

As we sat together in her friend's front room, I prescribed a long list of things to collect. It included two sticks measured from the crook of her elbow to the heel of her thumb, rye flour, wheat flour, salt, feathers, white, pink and blue flowers, metres of white, rose and sky-blue cloth, paints, pens, crayons, scissors, a penknife, paper, two pieces of old jewellery, glass beads, lemon balm, chamomile, lavender and some mead, the honey drink of the ancient inhabitants of Britain. I asked her to bargain or barter, beg or ask for as much as she possibly could; the more involved and complex the task the more it took her into ritual space, and out of her unhappy state. It also took her out into community, and when we are out of alignment we often tend to isolate ourselves.

Meeting again at her friend's house, we sat together at a kitchen table and I opened the ritual, talking Becky through the process and explaining everything as we went along. Having asked her to lay out all her objects, I then asked her to create two stick-figures, one masculine and one feminine, a pair of little fetishes no longer than her forearm. Each was precisely and exactly made, with the greatest of care, and each was storied and personalised in the making, as she imbued both figures with her breath and energy. As she worked her full story came out: her desire for a daughter and her difficult relationship with her own mother. Gradually the two figures took shape with their own distinct little faces and characteristics. I then talked her through the complex but beautiful process for 'creating a soul', of making an object that represented both the essence and the potential of her unborn child. This 'soul' was layered and layered until such time as she had a small cloth bag, filled with rye flour for nurture, salt for preservation, jewels for what is precious, lemon balm for love, chamomile for purity and lavender for health. Next I gently asked her to wrap the figures she had made, one in rose and one in sky-blue cloth, and to tie the soul to the two figures, who now clearly represented the male and female halves of her baby's undeveloped personality. Finally she bound all three together, making them one, swaddling it all in the full length of white cloth.

Becky, who had been getting quieter and quieter as the process unfolded, stopped before wrapping the finished object together. "It's my baby, isn't it?" she said. My silent nod witnessed her truth and she started to cry.

This moment of realisation has parallels in both theatre and therapy. There is the coming together of weeks of preparation and gathering; the sudden comprehension of the various objects and actions that have gone into the ritual; and the convergence of all four kinds of knowing (intellectual, physical, emotional and spiritual) in one moment. Like the point of catharsis in a tragedy or the sudden clear insight in therapy, we see a kind of fulcrum in any deep ritual which I have come to think of as the ritual shift.

The ritual shift can come as a slow discovery or a sudden download. The defining factor is the involvement of a bodily understanding and, often, a physical change in the manner or demeanour of the individual, a kind of general re-alignment that, like the crossing of any Rubicon, has a clear 'before' and 'after'. The important thing about the ritual shift is that it needs to be acknowledged and locked into the body, either by an anchoring action or object, or by an emotional experience that confirms the moment, locking it into the body-memory.

And so it was with Becky. It suddenly seemed that we both knew exactly where we were, and precisely what we needed to do. When I left her for a while to spend time with her 'daughter', she smiled softly, and without any self-consciousness, was able to say the things she needed to say to her re-creation of the baby that she had lost all those years before. A while later we drove out to a spot that we had agreed and, amidst yew trees and 'churchy' shrubbery, we gave her lost baby the rite of burial that it had lacked. As we did this I was struck by Becky's extraordinary dignity. Although she had cried from the moment of the ritual shift, and held her baby as if she would never give it up, she instinctively grasped the significance of the ritual and was able to lovingly place her sad little bundle of cloth, flour and sticks in its grave, and say the goodbyes she had always yearned to say, with a quiet grace. As we came away we agreed that she now had a place to go to, should she ever need to commune with her lost daughter.

These then are profound rituals we lack in our culture. Their absence leaves many of us both entangled *and* bereft, and I believe that, regardless of spirituality or morality, the more of these rituals we create, or re-instate, the better our psycho-spiritual and emotional health. Be they for people made redundant after a lifetime's service to an uncaring employer, or for lonely expatriates permanently stuck in the limbo of exile, we can once again find ways to create healthy completions and closures where they are lacking.

~

The other kind of ritual that I am often asked to perform is the ritual of the troubled soul: the atonement ritual and its many variants. In the absence of the confessional or any public means to express our regrets, we have reached a point in our culture where many of us carry an oppressive weight of guilt and shame without any means of getting past it. Troubled-soul rituals are common in various indigenous traditions, which understand how we accumulate grief and shame in our lives and the necessity of occasional purges. Sadly in the West, our fear of pain and suffering has got us to the point where we either shun these kinds of rituals completely or try to turn them into a *positive* experience. This means that, outside the therapy room and the confessional, much pain remains unaddressed and unhealed.

Pete was a sound engineer. He had done some silly things and got himself into hot water, and had actually been arrested and released pending a decision about whether to prosecute over something that he may or may not have done, which could be construed as criminal, or gullible, or just plain stupid, depending on the way the authorities viewed the issue. Much was shrouded in mystery, but it was clear that someone had been hurt. Pete was potentially in real trouble. He was sent to me by a friend, a therapist whom he had consulted and who knew the kind of work that I was doing. I agreed to talk to him about a ritual.

When Pete arrived, he was polite if reserved, and clearly very intelligent, but he was also slightly aloof, disembodied, even absent. My guess was that he lived in his head and didn't 'do' emotions, and that the stress of his situation was getting to him. That said, he got to the point pretty quickly and asked for my help. We talked for a while and he explained the situation. I couldn't really get a handle on him. Was he 'covering the bases', trying to wriggle out of something by doing a ritual which he had heard was effective, or did he genuinely feel the need to clear the past and make amends? I asked a few questions. He wasn't exactly obstructive but he wasn't giving anything away either. To put it plainly, he was a bit shifty.

I decided to tell him of my dilemma – that I wasn't confident about his motivation. He shuffled around and sounded evasive, which did nothing to put my fears at rest. Eventually I said that I would set up a ritual for him, but that I would reserve the right to stop the proceedings if I felt that either of us were drifting out of integrity. Pete nodded uncomfortably.

I set up an extensive and I must say quite demanding list of things for him to get and do before the ritual, and we contracted to meet soon as, for legal reasons, time was pressing. On the appointed evening we met at his neat and tidy home in the countryside, and I saw that he had done everything that I had asked, thoroughly, precisely and effectively. He hadn't asked any questions, as people often do, but had simply acquired what he needed to acquire, exactly as instructed.

I explained the journey of the next twelve hours and described the early stages of the all-night ritual, in which he was going to express in word, deed and making, his feelings of remorse – assuming he had them – around what had happened, regardless of the legal niceties. I then talked him through the making of a soul-blót offering: a representation of his soul, which he was eventually going to sacrifice, by giving it to nature as a kind of decoy.

The sacrifice of a decoy-fetish is a common tribal solution in these kinds of difficult situations. The perception is that the world of spirit is full of 'hungry ghosts', and has as much malign energy as good. Thus we put ourselves at risk when we interact with The Invisibles from a place of vulnerability, as Pete was about to do. In a secular European context, a soul-blót serves as a decoy, a representation of the individual's endangered soul or psyche (or their integrity or aspiration for example). Either way, the sacrifice of the decoy-fetish serves to 'meet' the threat by providing a representation of the individual, in lieu of their own precious soul. This is usually reinforced by repeating a simple mantra along the lines of, "Please accept this gift and leave me alone." The tribal understanding is that the spirits, who have a delight in objects to which feeling or creativity is attached, will readily 'eat' such an offering and refrain from eating the individual.

As I spoke, I noticed that Pete was edgy, even nervous. By the time we began to make things in preparation for the night ahead he was as taut and tense as a piano wire. I slowed things down deliberately, explaining everything I was doing, as if he were a visitor from another planet. I noticed that he was filling up with feeling, and on the edge of tears. "Now breathe on your soul-blót and make it yours," I said. "And if you should shed a tear, so much the better. It's good to add tears to your soul-blót."

It was as if he just needed permission. For a while he silently wept, wiping his tears on the cloth-bound decoy that he was making. Long, pregnant silences only deepened things as he gave himself over to the ritual. Slowly, he began to express his regret. As he began to speak, I saw that he wasn't trying to pull the wool over my eyes at all. He was just another isolated, lonely man who'd had no practice in community, or sharing.

We left to greet the dawn on a cold, wet, miserable morning; walking and slipping over muddy fields towards a dim hillock on the lightening horizon. Pete had certainly done his homework in finding a suitable place to offer up his soul-blót. We could have stepped straight into the pages of an Arthurian romance, standing as we were in a dank meadow leading towards a long-deserted castle mound, the kind of forlorn and lonesome place that villagers would have shunned for hundreds of years. Pete seemed withdrawn, and I feared that he might have climbed back into his shell but, when the moment came to place his soul-blót in the ground, he surprised me by sinking unbidden to his knees on the sodden turf, and speaking with heart-wrenching authenticity. "Forgive me. Please take this offering in my place. I'm *so* sorry."

It is so rare for modern people to get down on their knees. In our secular society, with our egos and individuality, we have no space for surrender, still less contrition. To see Pete speaking from such a place of humility and submission was deeply moving. I added my silent tears to those of this troubled and lonely man.

Finally, I helped him to his feet, and we chanted towards the thin misty sunrise, to help Pete to face the future with all that it might bring. (He was later to find that the police had decided not to prosecute.) As we stood there, with me chanting away purposefully, and Pete still clearly touched by the experience, we saw a movement ahead of us. Out of a tree, for no apparent reason and quite out of character, a buzzard flew straight towards us and over Pete's head, peeling away into the morning. Pete's look of awed astonishment spoke volumes.

An indigenous medicine man or woman would see a clear and specific signal in this physical response from what David Abram calls the more-than-human world. And time and again – even when I've been in states of weary disinterest – the environment seems to comment on rituals and even add to them. The secular part of me knows that a couple of quiet figures in a landscape are likely to draw the curiosity of a lazy but hungry buzzard, but the lost and yearning part of me is likely to see a blessing or a gift as such a majestic creature swoops out of the dawn and passes overhead.

These kinds of deep rituals don't need to be complicated, but they can't be entered into casually. In alignment rituals, or any ritual designed to heal, we are often working with wounded or shamed parts of our psyches or souls. As a badly burned returnee soldier once said to me, "It was as if I left my soul behind." Having been through a twenty-five year process of 're-enchantment', I have learned when to create ritual and when to suggest the services of a therapist or a doctor but I believe that with care and love, and the help of our communities, we can provide individuals with re-aligning or healing rituals that can bind up our wounded souls and restore us to a kind of balance.

~

Mary arrived during the afternoon, prepared and ready. There was an air of quiet determination about her and a sense of decisions having been made. She had a problem. She had lost the sight of one eye to toxoplasmosis and medical ineptitude. And she was afraid she was going to lose the other.

We had already talked about what she might want in a ritual. I had pointed out that I have no special powers, and that I would not be approaching a ritual in the expectation of *curing* her medical condition. That said, I thought I could help her in another way and we had agreed a ritual, which she had entered some six weeks earlier, when I sent her a long, long list of things to cut, gather, barter, buy and collect – including one genuine eagle feather. Once again the sheer complexity of the list got her into ritual space long before we met at my house. This is how she later described the experience:

> I was intrigued by the seven, flat, water-worn stones. I resolved to get them from distinct places, all with their own unique story and conditions. The rest looked straightforward enough, with the singular exception of 'one eagle's feather – genuine'. Where do you find one of those?

Some weeks later she had tracked one down to a falconry rescue centre.

Seeing Mary in front of me, nervous, anxious, and yet so committed that she had been prepared to track down a hard-to-find eagle's feather rather than simply buy one on the internet, I was struck by the way people instinctively reach for ritual, no matter how hard its tasks, as a way of addressing their problems. People have come to me for rituals that have helped them through all manner of individual crises and difficulties but I would never dream of offering a 'cure' to any kind of physical problem. I would invariably recommend that the person go to see a doctor. However, what people are commonly seeking when they come to someone like me is something else, something extra that is no longer obtainable from busy doctors or even from priests. What people often want in these cases is the practised attention of another soul, and through that attention a greater, deeper, wider connection to the natural healing of the world around them. This re-alignment can serve as shift enough to change a person's attitude towards their life to the point where a particular condition is no longer an unmanageable issue, at which point – be that as placebo, psychological counter-measure, distraction, or initiatory rite – the ritual has done its job. A medicine man or woman, of course, would say that the spirits have responded to a cry for help and that a rip in the fabric of the world has been repaired.

We began with the setting up of a shrine in my kitchen and then an invocation under the stars. My aim was to start by bringing Mary back in, if possible, to a place of trust and belonging, which would benefit her on a host of levels. This is how Mary experienced it:

> My memory of that evening is hazy. There was a vast, empty, scrubbed kitchen table awaiting. Almost everything I had brought for the ritual got unloaded onto this generous foundation; a huge landscape of ingredients, in a combination never seen before. It was like we were cooking up a spell, and I guess, effectively, we were!

We worked up a humdinger of a recipe ... I didn't half make a mess! Out of this mess my soul emerged, tied to a substantial stick. The whole thing was wrapped in white cloth and had a sling attached so that I could wear it next to my heart. I was to sleep with it and keep it with me throughout the ritual.

We went to bed early in preparation for a pre-dawn start the next day. I laid my soul on the bed as I changed out of my clothes. It looked kind of vulnerable lying there. As though wrapped in a winding sheet, yet to be brought back to life.

By the time she went off to bed filled with the ritual and ready to dream, Mary was visibly moved, as so many are, by the defenselessness and fragility of her soul-blót, which she held closely to her as she might a baby. Waking long before dawn we headed off to a fast-running local brook for the next part of the ritual.

It's very dark and very, very quiet. The whispering of the stream gets louder and louder. We are now at the edge. William beckons me further. The need for waterproof shoes is now becoming apparent to me. I am to step into the middle of the stream and find a secure footing. The water is shallow but the force is surprising so it takes a bit of balancing before I feel steady. My feet register cold as the water scrambles around them and I am enveloped into the sound of the stream. Casting my offerings onto the water, grateful for the cover of the stream's voice. I can see more easily where I have taken and not returned; where I have used with impunity, leaving things depleted, out of whack, unbalanced. The stream is glistening in the moonlight; the water cold, clear and true. It's chastening and invigorating, harsh but purifying.

As we finished this part of the ritual, I saw that Mary was changing, settling into the ritual process – more than just 'getting it'. "Where to now?" she asked, back at the car.

"Grey Hill," I said and we headed off towards one of the highest points in the area. This was to be the hardest and most exacting part of the ritual, involving an 800ft climb. The idea was to blindfold Mary while telling her Hyemeyohsts Storm's Jumping Mouse[23] story about the little mouse who gave away both eyes, while leading her to the very top of Grey Hill and taking off the blindfold as the sun rose over the far horizon, across the Severn Estuary. From my point of view it was important to fold the site into the ritual too. In lieu of the Sacred Mountain of the story, I was leading Mary, while sightless, to a remarkable sacred spot, a high place of ancient stone circles and imposing viewpoints, that had been used for ritual purposes for over four thousand years. Mary takes up the story:

Dawn was due at 06.23. William led me to a track and I began to follow him up the hill. The path was well worn and flanked by large bushes and trees preventing any view or perspective. As we climbed, he told me the story of Jumping Mouse.

You know, it was just a story. But William was telling this story – to me – and we were here because I had lost the use of my left eye. When Wolf asks Mouse for his second eye, I went cold and clammy. I found myself staring at my feet and, as the story unfolded, I felt leaden with dread. I accepted the blindfold passively. The remaining steps were taken completely in the dark. The story reached its climax as we reached ours. William removed the blindfold as we arrived at the top of Grey Hill at exactly 06.23. Dawn shot out across the countryside. The sky seemed so close. Clouds scudded against a pallid blue and the sun revealed the bounty of five counties.

Mary gasped as she stood atop the highest point of Grey Hill, and then sank into a quiet reverie, taking everything in.

The last part of the ritual involved her returning her sacrificial gifts to nature and then taking some time to go off alone and 'talk to the universe' and what she called 'the-powers-that-be'. She came back looking calm and yet very determined.

There's something about tucking into breakfast that makes life feel completely normal no matter how odd or eccentric your recent activities have been. So William and I ate our muesli and eggs at the now innocent-looking kitchen table, chatted about this and that and enjoyed the sunlight streaming in. More instructions for my final return home. And then a pause. "William, what was the eagle's feather for?" I asked.

"Ah," he said. "That's for me. Think of it as a trade."

I took the long scenic route home. It was a beautiful day and my heart was over-flowing with gratitude and awe at what we had done together. I never questioned how it would all turn out. It was now in the lap of the Gods.

Three and a half years later and Mary is living a very different kind of life. She says she is far more relaxed and is currently taking time with her husband to explore the waterways of Europe. I contacted her recently and asked, now that she had some distance and perspective, for her reflections on her ritual.

There have been big changes since. I am happier, healthier and more accepting of myself than I can remember at any other time, more able to tolerate peace.

I think the ritual helped me to integrate the experience [of losing my eye] fully and move on from it. The Jumping Mouse story as we climbed Grey Hill helped me place the loss and sacrifice into my life journey. Above all I believe it prevented me from creating some kind of crippled identity, another stamp in the Victim's passport. The ritual made me grateful too. It was a gift, which allowed me to experience gratitude, and that's a gift in itself.

Chapter Nine

Rookeries, Re-wiring and Relationship

Our job in this lifetime is not to shape ourselves into some ideal
we imagine we ought to be, but to find out who we are, and become it.
Stephen Pressfield: The War of Art

There is a part in any student that likes to think they have a special relationship with their teachers. The reality in my case was that, just like anyone else, much of my learning outside of books and tapes was done in open workshops and retreats. I was lucky that, when a number of medicine teachers from Africa and Central America came over to the UK to teach, I was unemployed and available to assist at their events. I became their gofer or runner, seeing to their comforts and helping them 'offline' before and after the events themselves. This gave me opportunities for conversations and discussions that sprang from the teaching and occasionally lead to further clarification and deeper learning – even personally prescribed rituals.

For some years then, I found myself in a deep learning process, serving as assistant and organiser to a spread of teachers, all of whom were adept at building communitas and creating the kinds of liminal spaces where deep change and learning can occur. I began to absorb layer upon layer of different teachings, drilling down through the sediment, in which I began to see patterns and commonalities of practice and thinking across linguistic and cultural divides. Not just about how to shape and hold ritual but how to interpret and integrate it too, and how to help suspicious yet curious individuals get to a point where their ritual instinct took over and they entered the process fully.

Needless to say I was also undergoing my own sea changes, as year upon year I underwent a series of initiations, rituals and rites of passage. One year

I would shed a burden around my family history, the next I would come face to face with my own naivety, or take a step forward in my creativity. Imperceptibly, I was morphing into someone else, putting together the pieces of a life, all the while overseen by my teachers and colleagues, and witnessed and supported by a whole community. What I began to see was that my life circumstance had made me a solitary. However, like any human being – and at a very deep level – I needed other people.

Tales of old European, Central American, and West African village life made me acutely aware of my own 'edge-of-the-village' nature. I belonged, and yet I was always somehow apart; uncomfortable in the midst of things, but passionately observing, as if from the outside. Many of the indigenous cultures I was studying recognised these outsider characters and saw them as valuable within their cultures.

One night I had a strange dream in which I was dragged by a group of troll-like creatures into a cave where I was held down on a huge anvil. I was then chopped into little pieces, or rather smashed like a piece of pottery, as the trolls broke me apart and then clumsily put me back together again with fumbling giant fingers. I was finally 'thrown out' into the morning, knowing that bits of me were missing, laying somewhere on the floor of the cave.

I'd read enough at this point to know about the "Healer's Dream": the prophetic dream in which healers are chopped up and restored minus the bit of themselves they could never heal in others.[24] This dream unsettled me as – for all my growing interest in ritual – I had no sense of myself as a healer and tended to be deeply suspicious of those who claimed the title. I therefore took this to one of my teachers, who was in London at the time. He seemed to take the whole thing in his stride. It appeared that this was a common dream amongst shamans, but also amongst artists. It certainly didn't sign me up, as a 'shaman's apprentice', to years of study in a far off cave. "Of course you're a shaman," he said. "All artists are shamans. The bits the giants forgot are the poems and books you will never write."

~

I soaked up my various teachers' insights like a sponge. Their ways of doing ritual were as different as the continents that bore them. Some were flamboyant, outgoing and showman-like; others more internalised, withheld and decorous. To a man – and woman – they were intensely observant, cautious and precise, and though some of them professed a kind of folksy village wisdom, they were all, without exception, respectful and understanding of our troubles and dilemmas in the West, even as they tried to unhitch us from our consumerist ways and patriarchal thinking. Some, inevitably, I was closer to, and some I have drifted away from since, but at the time, I now see, I was being granted something special and life-changing, not so much by direct 'downloading', as by osmosis, the gentle absorption of their beliefs and ways of being, as if through the skin.

Between them they re-introduced me to the rapture of being alive. In a series of nature-based rituals, public and private, over a period of years, they opened up a way for me to reconnect with that boundless sense of belonging that children feel with the natural world around them. The late mythologist Joseph Campbell once spoke to American journalist and commentator Bill Moyers about our way of interacting with the world. "People say that what we are seeking is a meaning for life," said Campbell. "I don't think that's what we are really seeking. I think what we're really seeking is an experience of being alive, so that our life experiences on the purely physical plane will have resonance within our innermost being and reality, so that we actually feel the rapture of being alive."[25]

I had experienced this whole-being immersion in life as a child, but like many of us, I had had my natural bond to the living, responding world educated (and occasionally beaten) out of me, not least at an English preparatory school. By the time I had spent twenty years living and working in the heart of London, I was as effectively dead to the world around me as if I had never experienced it. Fortunately, indigenous peoples the world over have maintained their sensory attachment to the planet, to their communities, and the world around them. The medicine teacher's wholly lived and instinctive union with their bodies, their villages, and with nature reignited my own guttering flame of connection. It spoke to the child-like, primal belonging that I had once felt in what had once been rural Mid-Hertfordshire: a wooded and pastured area that, in my lifetime, has become lost forever to housing estates, motorways and shopping malls.

One dry afternoon on one of these workshop retreats in the South of England, our group of thirty or forty seekers was told to go out into nature for an hour or so, to find a sound that we could adopt as our own, according to what attracted us, or *spoke to our soul*. We were also tasked to learn the sound and bring it back to the village – the instant workshop community that we had formed – where we were to announce our new-found 'sound signature' before the whole community. This was medicine-teacher-speak for "get out there and let *it* get to work on *you*".

I trooped out with the other participants and wandered off fairly aimlessly (as an assistant or gofer these occasions tended to be welcome opportunities to relax before the next round of setting-up or re-organising). I soon found myself completely alone in scenery not unlike my remembered childhood landscape of pasture and mixed woodland, separated by hedges and sunken lanes. An old oak stood in a meadow, on the brow of a hill, drawing me on. From beneath its branches I saw that, on the other side of the lea, there was a copse of mixed limes and sycamores, with one or two tall and graceful ash trees. What caught my attention and rooted me to the spot, however, was the fact that the entire copse had become a sizeable and noisy rookery. I was immediately overtaken by memories of the rookeries that topped the mighty elm trees of my childhood: the raucous, squabbling rookeries that dominated the skyline, bringing a rumbustuous parallel busyness to the very heart of the village. Most of all I remembered the haunting image of rooks trailing their way homeward down winter sunsets, their homing calls building to cries of welcome and recognition, eventually stilling as they found their twiggy nests and settled for the night.

Putting adult thoughts of embarrassment or foolishness aside I ran down the lea and up towards the rookery, which exploded in alarm as I knew it would, only to reconstitute itself as the rooks recognised me as no real threat. I stood looking up at the rooks' metropolis, noting once again the sophistication and subtlety of their caws and chuts, their mutterings and cries. As I watched, the community was joined by the usual afternoon stragglers, who circled and landed in their ones and twos, warily watching me watching them, all of us listening intently.

As I stood there in the calm of the afternoon, I became aware of the subtleties of the discourse going on in the tree-tops and the complexity of the relationships being played out in the community above me. As a kid, I had taken such vibrant presences as a given. But having spent the intervening decades in a kind of urban exile I had become increasingly isolated and cut off from the avian world. For an hour or so, I stood and watched, even as I was being watched, entering a reverie in which I absorbed every sound and movement that floated above me.

I have a sense that I was being rewired, plugged in once again to a deeper knowing. Not an intellectual understanding, still less a technical or scientific knowledge, but a sensory whole-body-knowing that radically realigned my relationship with the living world around me, and the very idea of community. I somehow shifted back from a detached and alienated "I-It" view of things, where I saw myself as separated from, and unhappily above, a world and its denizens in which everything and everyone was a thing or an object, to a lived and relational, some might even say sacred, "I-Thou"[26] view of life, in which I had renewed contact with a living world where everything was communal and interrelated, and consequently in relationship with me.

My childhood opened up like a picture book, somewhere in my chest. The places that I had known, Brocks Wood and Crackendell, the Mimram and Water End, returned to me as body memories, as did the old folk of my village. Dew-spangled spiders' webs hung on autumn hawthorns; the scent of wild garlic under vivid green hazels, and the whispering tingle of corn on my hands as I ran down rows of summer barley all came back to me in a rush and a wave. And everyone and everything was full of stories, and I was filled to the brim again with the wholly embodied yet un-thought learning of childhood.

I returned to the community, where the men and women were already separated into groups and facing each other. One by one, I heard the women start to ululate, whisper or hiss to the assembled company. What might have begun as an exercise in observation or attention soon settled into something else, as the women overcame their embarrassment and tried to get their deeply personal sounds across to the men opposite. Gradually the recital became more and more moving as, woman by woman, we were granted glimpses of unspoken but clearly expressed beauty, kindness or even hurt. By the time the men began their offerings in return, an air of acceptance and gentle respect had permeated the group. We really *were* becoming a community. I remember hearing the high-pitched and lonesome sound of a buzzard, the raucous crow of a cockerel, and the rocketing of a pheasant, which was soon followed by gentle cooings from a collared dove and the high whistling *kleese-kleese* of the swallow. Like the women before them the men, in their own particular way, found an un-worded eloquence that spoke to the community, soul to soul.

When my turn came I cawed the homing caw of the rook, which gradually morphed, as I worked my way down the line of women in front of me, into a general corvid cry for belonging, a crow-like sound that echoed in my nasal passage: part raven's honk, part crow's harsh demand, part desperate chick-like need to be heard. By the time I had reached the last few women I was 'crow-baby', unable to communicate because of my childhood defect, my lack of a soft palate. I was scared and afraid and desperately in need of the love to be found in a kind pair of eyes. And miraculously I got it. My hopeless, insistent "gnarghk-gnarghk-gnarghk", like all the other sounds that spoke from people's souls, touched the hearts of those I called out to. And being human they expressed themselves through their eyes. Without exception these sometimes shy, sometimes awkward women responded to my wounded croaking, and gave me back, in their compassionate looks, the healing love of the world and of true community.

When the last of our sounds had worked its way through the group, we all called out together. A vast and garrulous forest-full of noises: bird calls and rustlings, chirrupings and rattlings, waving, flapping, calling out and fundamentally belonging.

That night, as I sat apart, listening to the easy conversations of the men and women across the room, I became aware of another deep change within me. I no longer wanted, nor needed, to be alone. I had always imagined that 'sorting myself out' would somehow make me more eligible, yet I was well into my forties and, despite some hard work, unable to form a meaningful relationship. Working with the shamans was adding to my skills as a ritualist, but I was still woefully under-skilled when it came to finding myself a life-partner. I liked to think of myself, at that time, as a solitary artist, or some kind of wounded romantic, but in my heart of hearts I knew that I was just lonely. Sitting there that night, I knew I wanted my life to be different from now on, but I didn't know how to begin. Fortunately, things were about to happen that would change all that.

~

I had been doing a lot of ritual that summer, maybe too much: leading events for Wild Dance; co-leading the latest Rites of Passage week; exploring quarter-day ceremonies and nature rituals with a friend, Steve Banks; holding weddings and funerals as a celebrant for friends. By the time one of the shamans came to London again, to lead two consecutive weekend workshops, I was well and truly stuck in liminal space, a vague and woozy, slo-mo space where I felt like I was wrapped in cotton wool.

I think there's more of this kind of thing out in the world these days than we realise. When we enter ritual space we get a sense of 'super-reality', of deepening. It's attractive and can hold us rapt. It's a kind of enthralment, which interestingly used to be called 'glamour'. It can be, psycho-spiritually and emotionally, very sticky. The great religions of the world understand this fully and shut down their ceremonies with suitable attention to parting prayers and blessings, gestures and farewells so that their communities can return to their everyday doings, and leave the magic of sacred space behind, where it belongs.

That's not to say that everyone's started doing rituals, of course. Far from it. But with the decline of religion and the rise of mass entertainment, we find ourselves more prone to getting stuck in these 'magical' moods and states. If you've ever come out of a movie that had an unsatisfactory or incomplete ending, you'll know what I mean. Part of you still feels engrossed in the experience while another part of you feels cheated or somehow 'wrong', still stuck in the imaginal world of myth and story. This is often no more than a brief mood or an inkling, but it can linger for days.

On a grander scale, stadium rock and the growing number of music festivals often fail to close things down sufficiently for people to leave properly 'grounded', to safely return to the everyday world of handbrakes and hamburgers, headlights and homework. The sheer high of coming into contact with one's cultural 'gods' or rock and roll 'idols', of being a part of their quasi-religious ceremonies, can have all the power of a major ritual experience, though without the vital element of intention or conscious purpose. Thus the lines between sacred and ordinary spaces have become blurred in the modern world where personal devices can extend the experience of dissociation far beyond the original liminal experience.[27]

Either way, on that warm summer's evening in London, I was well and truly stuck in liminal space – vulnerable, emotional and unable to think straight. I was also exhausted and barely able to hold a conversation. After yet another full-on day of ritual preparation and community building, I was also desperately in need of some sleep. So, ducking out of a social evening with friends, I headed back to Swiss Cottage and my gloomy basement flat. On the way, realising that I was hungry, I stepped into a Greek taverna and ordered a kebab. And that's when things started to get weird.

To say I was alarmed would be an understatement. I'm pretty imaginative, but I'm not generally given to hallucinating, and, while I'm open to anything that might happen in ritual space, I tend to seek a rational explanation for anything odd that occurs outside rituals. Here I sat, mesmerised, in a busy restaurant, as the water in my glass on the table began to stir and move, seething and churning as if it were alive. I ate my kebab at record speed and returned home where, despite my need for sleep, I spent a restless night, anxious that I was going mad.

Early the following morning I approached my teacher and told him what had happened. He looked at me quizzically, his friendly concern replaced by the medicine teacher's attentive stare.

"Did you speak to it?"

"Er... No..."

"Well, it was speaking to you."

I felt like I was falling down a hole.

I was introduced to what appeared to be an altogether deeper level of personal ritual, the kind of thing that wizards and medicine women have been doing for individuals for thousands of years. At this level, where imagination, dreaming and healing practice blend into one, I was prescribed a solemn ritual that addressed the heart of my problem, by responding to the 'call' or warning I had recognised in my depleted state. The ritual addressed my increasingly pressing problems around connecting at the most intimate levels. It lasted for a long time – longer than any ritual I had previously experienced – and radically restructured my whole concept of relating and relationships. I was given the most exacting list of things to do and say. I did this ritual entirely on my own, and it involved as deep and challenging a look as I had ever taken at myself, and the way I related to others.

The fact was that my wiring around relationships was hopelessly compromised and shorting out all over the place. I had not realised this, but the universe certainly had. My relationships with women were coloured by a neediness that women seemed to pick up and, quite rightly, reject. As a consequence I was increasingly lonely, withdrawn and diminished. This was made worse by my historical relationship with my mother – I'd spent most of my life around her chasing a love that simply wasn't forthcoming. This made me even more desperate and useless around women, a classic narcissistic 'flying boy', in fact – nice, kind and rather useless. But had I actually done *harm* in relationship? Of course I had – at all levels. For all my niceness, I was a typically patriarchal product of boarding schools, work and my nice, polite yet broadly sexist upbringing. *Of course* I had done harm. I needed to make amends, through the ritual.

This is not the place to go into the 'how to' of such an elaborate ritual. It could fill a book in itself. It's enough to say that it brought me to a place of deep, whole-bodied realisation, where I found myself weeping tears of remorse for all the harm I had done to my mother, my female relatives, the wonderful old women of my village, old female teachers and mentors in the casino business, all the women that I had intentionally and unintentionally belittled or patronised. Then there was my *anima* as the Jungians call it, my own deep feminine soul if you will, which I had assiduously ignored and unwittingly degraded for years; minimising my skills and trashing my talents, so many of which lay on what we sometimes sneeringly call the feminine side of the ledger.

When I was finished, I carefully gave the ritual's paraphernalia back to nature and returned to my strangely lighter flat, where I tidied up and slept profoundly. When I awoke I didn't *feel* particularly different and yet I knew a seismic shift had occurred. I saw women differently, and men, and in some indefinable way I was different around others by being more aware of something more solid in myself. I knew that something had changed from the inside out. And I fully understood, as if for the first time, what I heard different teachers say more than once: "If you haven't fallen in love with your own soul, how can you possibly fall in love with another!" Two weeks later I was in a relationship.

Juliet was a powerful and loving woman whom I had met some while before and then foolishly shied away from. Many years later, she has changed my life beyond all imagining and I am still with her. Watching her from my writing table as she relaxes by the pond, I see a wise woman and a healer, a businesswoman and a teacher all rolled into one. I am astonished that she should still be with me, let alone have married me. I also know, beyond reasonable doubt, that it was a shaman's ritual that brought her fully into my life, and for that I am deeply indebted.

Chapter Ten

The Art of Smudge:
More than Smoke and Mirrors

Let me learn the lessons you have hidden in every leaf and stone.
Chief Yellow Lark

S omething bad happened yesterday. We came home to Albion Pond from an afternoon on the Maine Coast, where we had enjoyed the last of the summer and the first misty intimations of the fall. I foolishly opened a little flurry of e-mails, which had come in while we were having supper. One was from a colleague back home who had taken exception to something I had done while trying my hardest to serve him. His high tone, capital letters and exclamation marks, not to mention his air of spiritual superiority, caught me on the hop, shamed me deeply, and left me feeling wretched. A further exchange of explanations and half-apologies from his end did little to change my mood. I had stirred some long-dormant spite of his that had leapt out like a snake, to bite me and pass on its poison. I slept badly, spinning down through hurt-filled dreams. I awoke flushed and miserable, locked into old beliefs that left me feeling and behaving like a cowed and resentful nine-year-old. I could see what was happening to me, but felt powerless to change things. I was trapped in my unhappy past again.

I decided to smudge myself. Smudging is an age-old ritual that involves the purification of people and places with the smoke of particular plants, herbs and resins, each with their own distinctive scents and properties. On this occasion, I grabbed a bundle of freshly-dried cedar that I had been given recently, a turkey buzzard's feather that I had picked up, and a kitchen gas lighter. I then went out onto the deck overlooking the lake and performed a simple smudging ritual of purification that helped me to shake off the sticky, slimy feeling of being belittled and shamed. I held the intention to clear away the miasma of stale old feelings that had engulfed me, lit one end of the bundle of cedar, and began to pass the smoke over myself, wafting the feather to cover me from head to foot in the cedar's cleansing aroma. I also spoke of my feelings, and asked for them to be taken away, and that I be healed and protected from these kinds of hurtful attacks. As I did this I imagined the sticky shame and envy peeling away, pulled off and carried away by the deliciously aromatic smoke. In doing this I noticed that my face was still flushed with feelings of hot, toxic shame – I was literally shame-faced. So I spent extra time wafting smoke over my face and head, bathing my closed eyes, nose and mouth in the smoke, feeling it soothe, heal and, in my imagination, protect me.

As I was near the pond I finished my ritual with a dip in the water, a kind of watery version of what I had just done with the smoke. On a hot and sweltering day the water felt cool to my skin and left me feeling doubly cleansed. I returned to the cottage and sat at my desk, able now to work, fully present and free of the state that had dogged me since waking. I had smudged myself clean.

~

Velma is a small, quiet Native American woman who lives with her son in Maine. She is quick to smile and her voice has a gentle First Nation lilt that comes with hard lives and gracious acceptance. Velma's eyes haven't been so good lately, having endured three major operations, but she has regained her sight to the point where she can see well enough to show us round a part of her village, home of one of the W'abanaki tribes of northern New England. Meeting us, it seems, is just a matter of natural kindliness, and of honouring strangers despite her uncertainties. She leads us away from our rendezvous point overlooking the river, and proposes a walk along the village's Medicine Trail, a winding, shaded walk through medicinal herbs, mixed woodland, fallen trees, fungi and wildlife.

As we amble through the village, our talk turns to smudging and purification. Purification rituals using smoke, water or salt are common to most cultures, and are familiar to many of us, be that through dense clouds of joss sticks at Taoist temples in Hong Kong, the throwing of salt by sumo wrestlers, or the simple Judaic washing of hands before a Shabbat meal. The aim is to clear the individual or area of impurities – and by extension, spiritual, psychic, or energetic clutter – though from a lay perspective you could say that it simply serves to settle the individual or group into the right frame of mind, a useful bookmark to separate the time of ritual from the humdrum daily round. Over millennia, Native Americans have refined the use of smoking herbs like sage or cedar to a precise yet delicate art. Like the tea ceremony in Japan, it has become a cultural flag and icon. Personally, I've found that smudging with herbs or resin has a calming and centering effect, as well as being a direct call to reflection and seriousness.

I'm fascinated by the air of quiet gravitas that settles around Velma as she talks haltingly about her practice of smudging. There's a deep humility at work here, and something else, indefinable yet compelling, that has me wanting to learn from her, to bombard her with questions. Does she collect her own smudge? What herbs does she use? Can you pick it at any time?

"I will gather you some." In true indigenous style, Velma decides to show us by doing rather than talking. We head for a nearby stand of young flat cedar (*Thuja occidentalis*), which she gathers and uses for protection and cleansing, to drive out the negative and bring in the positive. "I use it when I'm praying, and to protect myself when things get bad." She walks round the cedar, appraising it, and finally addresses it from the north. "Right place to begin," she says.

What strikes me is Velma's deep respect for the plant she is addressing and her sense of being connected, not just to the plant itself, but to everything near it and around it, in it and on it. First we settle, and she addresses the flat cedar directly. She speaks quietly, telling the plant what it will be used for, asking the cedar to give itself for our benefit, and thanking it for this act of generosity. She then gently bends and leaves a gift, or sacrifice. In the W'abanaki tradition, this would usually be garden-grown, or at least local-grown, tobacco; in this instance, having come unprepared, she places a small coral bead that I have given her at the foot of the six-foot high shrub, in honour of my old European way of offering blót, the ancient Anglo-Saxon form of sacrifice, which I've told her about. I follow suit, quietly mouthing a genuine, heartfelt thank you.

Velma is scrupulously careful in gathering this bundle of cedar for me. She parts different fronds, and selects the pieces she deems most appropriate, moving from spot to spot to take each separate, hand-shaped piece. She carefully works round the lattice of spiders' webs that shows up clearly amongst the rich green fronds on this early autumn day. "Are the spiders dangerous round here?" I ask.

"No. I just don't want to disturb them," she replies matter-of-factly.

While she patiently and deftly collects the cedar, and works it into a loose bundle, we talk about the four sacred herbs of Native American lore: cedar, which protects; sage, which drives out the bad and the harmful; tobacco, the great activator and connector; and sweet grass, the sacred herb of Mother Earth, whose delicious scent reminds people of her kindness and generosity. We also talk about mugwort (wormwood), which is used by those seeking creativity, and lucid, even prophetic dreams.

Velma's life journey, through abusive relationships, dislocation and divorce, has brought her to a quiet place where she feels a special affinity to the protective and healing powers of cedar. Her quiet, offhand, "Oh, I use it for prayers" hides a deeper relationship within which she feels secure, protected and safe from harm. She holds the cedar gently between her two palms and hands it over to me with a radiant smile. I can't help but dip my head in thanks.

"How should I dry it?" I ask, cursing myself internally for sounding so pious about it.

"Oh, I just leave it on the dashboard of my Chevy. That dries it out good," she says with a twinkle.

Like many native people Velma has developed her own spiritual practice as she has moved from area to area, and nation to nation, as marriage and separation have decreed. Throughout, her life has been lived face-to-face with nature, the deep cold of winter and the mosquito-humming humidity of summer. She uses smudging as a regular, if not a daily practice, which helps and sustains her.

~

Over the years I've had an uncomfortable relationship with smudging. As I wrestled with my two-thousand-year-long inheritance of overly pious religiosity, and my own in-built perfectionism, I made all the usual mistakes of over-focus and fussiness. I understood smudging's value in 'setting the scene', but I hadn't really cottoned on to the fact that, before one can be healed, still less help another, one has to be cleansed of what Velma would call 'bad sickness'. This might be bad spirits, harmful energies or negative thought forms (and, yes, the pungency of sage or the delicacy of sweet grass really *can* change the way you think and feel, as I have found time and again). Smudging is a simple yet powerful 'pre-ritual', which helps the main ritual to work in a clearer, uncluttered way, without the psycho-emotional distortions of what we might otherwise bring to it. As a Native elder might say, you need to enter a ceremony with a clear heart, so that you can pray, chant, or walk in a sacred manner. It wasn't until I had been working with indigenous teachers for some while that I came to grasp the power of smudging and to realise that I could also use the occasion to focus my own attention where it needed to be – on the person I was smudging in the moment – inside and out.

Different medicine teachers have very different ways and preferences when it comes to smudging. Generally speaking, the Native American way is to use sage or other herbs while Central American practitioners from Mexico, Guatemala and elsewhere tend to use copal[28], a powerfully aromatic resin. South American practitioners sometimes burn Dragons Blood, a dried sap from the rainforest, or Palo Santo, a fragrant wood that is burned as an incense, like sandalwood. Over time I developed a liking for copal, though lately I have come to experiment with European resins, seeking a local equivalent that serves in place of lavender, and fits with our own traditions and needs.

And then, inevitably, each practitioner has their own manner of smudging, what we might think of as their own style. Some have a loose way of setting things up that covers for an intense and focused precision. This can involve a jolly, conversational way of preparing both site and participants, intercut with moments of penetrating observation, fierce attention, and most important of all, perhaps, a perceptible flow of energy from the smudger to the person they are smudging. Chatting away merrily to a group, for instance, they might meticulously set up and light a charcoal briquette[29] in a smudge bowl, or sea-shell, waiting for it to frost over with ash as it heated through. Next, they might cut off an amount of pliable, tacky copal. One shaman only used the finest, most sacred, gold copal, traded in the street markets of Guatemala, wrapped in corn leaves, that could scent a whole room. Having cut off exactly the right amount, he would place it precisely on the now-glowing charcoal, where the resin melted and gave off its pungent, aromatic and evocative smoke.

While some practitioners smudged people with meticulous care and intensity, concentrating on the person before them, others would smudge as if casually playing a musical instrument: not quite cool, not quite self-conscious, but a performance that drew people into the process nonetheless. As I watched my various teachers, what I began to see was that smudging was one of the activities that allowed a medicine teacher to employ their *showman* side, involving people, and settling them into the right frame of mind, while their *shaman* side made invocations to the particular gods they sensed and served. This quiet litany of muttered calls, part-prayer, part-chant, were incantations that happened to beguile the onlooker, while the smudger invoked The Other, whom they were contacting on our behalf. They were bringing two worlds together for the common good, using the shaman's influence to bless and heal.

One teacher I was especially fond of would go to great lengths to set this tone of present attention, making little animal yips and hollerings, as he addressed each individual, noting their emotional states and holding their attention as he made his way round the circle; wafting smoke over them, occasionally lifting an arm with his smudging feather or fan, tapping an individual on the shoulder, and dragging away negative energy (which is commonly believed to hide in the armpits and hidden places).

Occasionally an experienced practitioner would give an individual more time than others, though always somehow referring to the group as a whole. Or he might appear almost angry, as he paused by a visibly sick man, or a clearly worried woman. Then he would waft extra smoke at them, cutting and carving the air fiercely, tapping their heads, running the fan down their arms and ripping it away from them suddenly so that it whistled. At such times he might flick the fan violently downwards, shaking off some dark energy he wanted to draw out and throw to the earth.

Once, I saw a shaman stop by a sad young lad who had clearly been horribly shamed and still bore the scars. He paused, observing the downcast youth, and then swung into a kind of balletic 'smudge-dance', drawing back and arching his body, holding the fan in a great arc above him, shape-shifting into a birdlike pose and then growling and snarling from deep within his throat like some forest carnivore. He then pounced on the hurt – there's no other way of describing it – and ripped it out. Finally moving on with a tap of the fan and a friendly, "You need to smile more."

At the start of a ritual weekend or before a long and often complex ceremony, we would invariably take extra time to smudge the entire circle. Each and every person would get the right amount of attention, the appropriate and necessary amount of purification. What I saw was that, time and again, by investing extra time and energy into the smudging, the teachers, and increasingly their teams or those entrusted with the smudging, would have substantially altered the state of many participants before they had even entered the ritual they were about to do. They had also thoroughly prepared the ground for the forthcoming ritual, which, despite any apparent fooling around, or light-heartedness, they would be addressing with utmost seriousness.

Gradually, watching and practicing these various forms of smudging, I found a balance between religiously 'getting it right' and a laid-back comedic routine, so that smudging became a natural, 'un-thought', emotionally engaged, yet instinctive process that allowed what needed to arise to do so. In other words, it stopped me from being a stuffed shirt and allowed me to serve people through the act of smudging, and then get out of the way.

Getting out of the way in ritual, and certainly in smudging, is important. It gives The Other a chance to do its unknown thing, and allows more-than-human Creation an opportunity to come through and make its presence felt too. It's all too easy to impose oneself on a ritual, to play the high priest, and so stifle the natural flow of things, even while claiming to be in service. Shamans, by right of their initiation, tend to have dealt with this particular kink in their natures (even when they have big egos), but the rest of us, urbanised and sophisticated as we are, will always be prone to getting in the way. If we are to develop any kind of meaningful ritual practice, it's something we have to watch out for.

This is where the shaman versus showman sides of the ritualist begin to blur. As with any experienced artists, good practice leads to better 'performance', to the point where, in moments of grace, the practitioner simply steps out of the equation. This allows something truly extraordinary to happen, at the very point where the diverse yet complimentary 'magics' of theatre, art and healing meet. There's a paradox here. At our very best we are both there and not there. I have seen actors like Mark Rylance, who has a distinct and obvious personality, virtually vanish on stage when playing Hamlet, or Richard III, allowing Shakespeare's tragic intention to sweep through to shattering effect. Likewise, I have listened spellbound as Mitsuko Uschida at the piano, or Nigel North on the lute, have stepped aside to allow the artistic genius of Mozart or Bach to fill the room – as Salieri says of Mozart in Peter Shaffer's Amadeus, "So that it seemed to me that I was hearing the very voice of God."[30]

This vanishing act is not just limited to 'the greats' of course, it is happening in jazz clubs and comedy clubs, flamenco schools and dance classes any night of the week. Artists of every stripe and persuasion dip into and out of what we might call 'peak performance' time and time again, to our delight and their frustration. Stephen Nachmanovitch sums this up nicely in *Free Play*, his remarkable book on improvisation in life and art. "Spontaneous creation comes from our deepest being and is immaculately and originally ourselves. What we have to express is already with us, is us, so the work of creativity is not a matter of making the material come, but of unblocking the obstacles to its natural flow."[31] And that, of course, includes ourselves, our egos and our need to play a role. This is doubly true in ritual space, where our essentially improvised 'performance' is judged as much by its authenticity as by any standards of strict ceremonial behaviour or religious norms. Even in something as seemingly straightforward as smudging, this 'absence' of our egos can be vital. Getting out of the way allows the extraordinary to happen.

I once conducted the funeral of a dear friend, who had died of a brain tumour days after leaving one of our Rites of Passage retreats near Llanberis. Steve Stephens was a delightfully open-hearted man with a deep understanding of music, and an abiding love for his talented and creative family. His wife Sarah, son Lyall and daughter Erin decided that he should be interred on the mountainside in North Wales, overlooking the places where he had experienced life-changing initiations and moments of profound connection, both with other men, and with the landscape of the Carneddau, the mountains of Snowdonia. We gathered on a late September afternoon amidst tussocks of windswept grass, and piles of shattered slate, overlooking the still waters of Llyn Padarn, as three parallel ceremonies began simultaneously in Dorset, London and New Zealand. We gathered in a forlorn circle as our friend's hand-painted, cardboard coffin was carried to the graveside, and I found myself deeply moved as his mother, Edna, who was suffering from vascular dementia, was gently led, seemingly absent, into the circle.

This was no time for me to enter my own grief, however. I had a job to do. Our friend had always loved the creativity and fellowship of our rituals, which he and his son had attended, and I had been asked to perform a specifically Central American ritual invocation and smudging as part of the funeral service. I lifted my crock with its burning briquette and placed a large piece of copal on the hot charcoal, copal that I had been given for just such special occasions. It smoked profusely as I made an invocation to the cardinal directions. I began to smudge everyone in the circle, trying, despite my feelings (or perhaps because of them) to give myself over to the ritual, using the moment to bless those who had braved the day to say farewell to the lovely man who lay in his multi-coloured coffin. I worked my way around the circle, connecting where I could, comforting when possible in word and gesture, with smoke and touch. As I went along, I explained what I was doing for the benefit of those who had never experienced ritual before. I carried on, resolutely moving round the circle, steering the rickety wagon of the ritual. I blessed what needed to be blessed, and honoured what needed to be honoured: a sad face here, a brave smile there, an old friend moved to tears by shock and loss. And then I saw I was coming to Steve's mother.

Tiny and grey and seemingly unaware, she stood silent and withdrawn in this unfamiliar setting, waiting her turn with the infinite patience of the lost and bewildered. As I stepped round to face her I felt called to honour my friend by honouring her, here or not, to the utmost of my love and care. I added another lump of copal to the charcoal. And then, somehow, I got out of the way.

What happened was that I crouched before her, stood back and came right in again. Muttering away, I described her outline with the fan, moving up and down her arms and sides. I circled the fan and pulled with all my might, hearing myself chuckle as I felt the energy grip. "Erch!" Finally I circled her head in a gesture of blessing and let the fan come to rest, gently, just below her chin. Slowly she raised her head, and looked me in the eye.

"Thank you for what you are doing for my son," she said. Clear as a bell.

~

Velma, up on her icy river, with her bunch of protective flat cedar and her profound sense of belonging, showed me that smudging, like any ritual activity, can bring about a deep shift in one's perception of the world. It can benefit one's inner life, as much as meditation or yoga. And, when allied with a re-engaged respect for nature and an open heart, it can serve as a gateway to a life that is altogether more connected, more accepting, and more rewarding. Velma will, like us all, find her way in a difficult world, but unlike many of us, whatever comes, she will know herself a welcome and valued part of the whole. It's not just her practice of smudging, of course, but smudging surely helps.

Chapter Eleven

A Home for the Mystery: Shrines and Spirit Houses

Shrines at their simplest define a space where the work of ritual can occur.
Malidoma Somé

I've always been drawn to the magic of shrines. As a child I used, quite unconsciously, to make impromptu shrines by draping an up-ended stool with an old silk headscarf of my mother's and placing favourite objects inside. A little later, having discovered an early nineteenth century dump at the bottom of our garden, I graduated to an abandoned shed, which I filled with ancient green bottles, decorated shards of broken pottery and the precious skull of a muntjac, a small barking deer, which I had found in the woods. I spent hours on my own, setting up and arranging these 'installations', lavishing care and attention upon them, instinctively sensing some kind of 'magic' in them.

By the time I had been working in the casinos for twenty years, I had started picking up stones on walks (a shaman would have said that my village was speaking to me even then). After I crashed and burned, when my world seemed to be falling apart, I began noticing rounded stones on paths and beaches, bringing them back home, where I left them on windowsills and table tops. I didn't know what to do with them but I sensed that they had a hidden meaning. In a strange and inexplicable way, they were also a comfort. They were company.

What I was doing, however unwittingly, was gathering together the components of another shrine. *Ifa*, one of the great, earth-based spiritualities of Africa, teaches, in its practical way, that if you are confused about anything, a good tidy up in the home will bring clarity and sense out of confusion and disorder. The Dagara tradition meanwhile might say that my attraction to stones was a call from one of the Dagara elements, 'Mineral', which represents memory and remembrance. One summer's evening after I had revisited my village and placed the stones on the graves, I made a shrine. I had bought two large Japanese ceramic dishes, especially for the purpose, and I gathered all my stones together and placed each stone reverently upon one of the dishes. These great platters, filled with their rounded stones, have travelled with me from home to home for over twenty years now, and whenever I look at them I am still calmed and comforted, brought present to a host of images and memories, though oddly, each individual stone is losing its sense of reference to an individual moment. Like our dead, who are said to lose their individual personalities as they join the ancestors, they seem to be gaining in power whilst losing their identity.

Nowadays, all over the world, impromptu floral tributes and shrines are a commonplace at the scene of any atrocity or disaster. Having had countless traumatic images, from assassinations and car crashes to the collapse of the Twin Towers in New York, beamed into our living rooms, we feel present to these events and seek to make our human response by ritualising what is in truth a common and repetitive trauma.

This was never more evident than after the sudden passing of Diana, Princess of Wales. Waking up to the gruesome death of this world-famous, very public beauty, who died in such brutal, sordid circumstances, people found themselves in a common field of shock and grief that seemed to transcend both the passing of a public figure and the loss of a society beauty whom the media had made 'our own'. Vernacular commemoration was unleashed on a grand scale. People went in their tens of thousands to the gates of Kensington Palace, leaving bouquets, soft toys, condolence cards and bunches of flowers. Some were moved to wondering silence and others to vituperative wrath. A backlash soon developed in the broadsheet press with people accusing others in the most contemptuous terms of sentimental hysteria, emotional fascism, expressive incontinence and downright insincerity. As is common at funerals the world over, we were seeing the best of ourselves, and the worst.

Amongst the detractors and those who wished to distance themselves from the 'common herd' the assumption was that, firstly we were all being coerced into feeling in a certain way, and secondly that the feelings expressed were somehow false, or at the very least 'over the top' and somehow indecorous or unseemly.

I was in London the day before the Princess's funeral, preparing to support Richard Olivier and Mark Rylance at a Globe Theatre workshop. Having heard that something truly extraordinary was developing around the royal palaces, Richard, a friend Mark Goodwin, and I decided to take a look for ourselves; three mature, middle-class men, none of us particularly attached to Princess Di, but intrigued to see what all the fuss was about. It was a still, warm, late summer evening, and we walked along chatting amiably, until, quite suddenly, we were hit by a wall of scent that came from the flowers in the Mall, which must have been over a quarter of a mile away. Silent now, we passed between St James's Palace and Marlborough House, picking up the sense of respect and wonder from those who were walking away. What greeted us as we turned into the Mall was breathtaking. Under the double row of plane trees that runs the length of the Mall from Admiralty Arch up to the Victoria Memorial, there were literally hundreds of shrines. Each tree seemed to have grown its own little sanctuary, with cloths laid out and flowers in vases, while the iron fencing that usually marked the outer boundaries of St James's Palace and Clarence House was hung with laminated photographs, framed pictures, messages of heartfelt commiseration and millions of flowers. The whole was lit by thousands upon thousands of candles, which outshone the dappled light of the Mall's street lamps up amongst the trees.

Apart from the flowers, the most memorable thing to me was that these hundreds of shrines were nearly all attended by women: Asian women in coloured saris and shalwar kameez; African women in exuberantly printed gowns and headdresses; Australian women with their backpacks and their boots; women from Soho's Chinatown; Black English mothers with their daughters from the inner city and groups of sixth-form girls from the suburbs and the home counties. All were impeccably turned out, all perfectly and decorously behaved. There was no wailing and gnashing of teeth, no rolling on the gravel. The odd woman comforted another as a wave of grief passed through but there was nothing to scare or offend, nothing out of place. As a man I felt that I had been granted a glimpse of some ancient mystery. I felt privileged to be there.

Not so the 'shrine haters' who thought the whole thing intrusive, inappropriate and above all impertinent. They felt manipulated, imposed upon, forced to feel in a certain way, and accept a public presence they neither subscribed to nor believed in. Their oddly rageful responses seemed to miss the fact that they really did have a choice, and that the whole idea of these kinds of shrines is that they are temporary. They are invariably tidied away, or left to return to nature. The issue rumbled on for years. Tracy Potts, of Nottingham University[32], quotes an article in The Guardian by the writer and broadcaster, Muriel Gray, who in writing a valid enough piece about the inconsiderate building of memorial cairns on Scottish mountainsides took the following excoriating side-swipe at shrines and shrine builders in general.

> *Since the days, eight years ago, when crowds of social misfits dumped rotting heaps of cellophane-wrapped flowers outside Kensington Palace when a woman they had never met died in a car accident, the repulsive habit of leaving makeshift memorials wherever one pleases has grown to epidemic proportions. There's barely a street corner in any town or city that doesn't sport a withered pile of cheap bouquets to mark some horrible accident or violent crime, and even worse, the wild places of Britain are becoming littered with a collection of cairns and plaques that are considerably more permanent than the petrol-station-bought chrysanthemums and grimy teddy bears crucified on metal crash barriers.[33]*

Shrines are not arbitrary or accidental assemblages of sentimental dross and detritus. They are tangible, often deeply-felt evidence of humanity's need to physicalise acts of remembrance. They arise in the midst of life and serve as both focus and reminder. At their best they can hold astonishing accretions of power and emotions, and at the very least, they allow the better parts of us to make gestures toward the lost, the archetypal and The Other, gestures that reflect our individual need to express or process emotion at times of grief and shock.

Like most of us you probably have a collection of precious or prized items at home that have found their way onto your mantle piece, desk or sideboard. They tend to have a great but private value and meaning: a souvenir Eiffel Tower from Paris, a photo of a long-dead friend, a horrible little pot made at school by a beloved child. Gathered together, these things make a shrine.

The word shrine comes down to us from the Old English word, *scrīn*, meaning a chest, or a reliquary. Shrines can be of any size and shape, indoors or outside, enclosed or otherwise. They don't have to be specifically religious, though they often hold a religious, spiritual or 'Otherly' quality.

Ron Pyatt, a master shrine-builder in his time, was always adamant that the shrines in his rituals be open to all interpretations, religious or otherwise. What really mattered to him was that the shrine provided a kind of inner access. "Take the ritual device of a shrine," he said when interviewed by Steve Banks for the men's magazine, *Achilles Heel*. "One of the things a shrine does is mark a place to attend to. It is a place to be reminded of what truly matters to you, what is in your heart. On your shrine you can place anything, from a goddess or god whose qualities you value and hope to possess, to pictures of people you love and cherish. Its effectiveness is not dependent on beliefs: it goes with the territory of being human." [34]

Shamans the world over hold that shrines and altars are the homes of spirits and gods, and that they can collect and hold a great deal of energy. At their best they can gather and store the psychic energy of a community or a generation.

This talk of energies can be difficult for those who reject the notion of 'psychic energy' or power in this context. However, consider what happens when you go for a walk out in the cold holding a stone in your hand, in a pocket. When you place the stone on your cold cheek, you feel an exchange of heat, of energy. Energy moves and yet energy cannot be destroyed. Well, a medicine man, a yogi, or a Taoist master would say much the same with regard to *mana*, *prana*, or *qi* (being Polynesian, Indian and Chinese forms of life-force, energy). We see its effects and we know it is there. Like electricity, it is real enough to us, and it can be harnessed, deposited or stored. Curiously they are no longer alone in thinking this. For some years now scientists in a number of disciplines around the world have been reporting on well-managed experiments that fly directly in the face of current beliefs and assumptions held by biology and physics. Newton, it seems, no longer reigns supreme as quantum physics and noetic science continue to blur the lines, and open up the spaces, between thought forms and matter, prayers, objects, organisms, and emotions. [35]

~

Nowhere are these energies courted and engaged more diligently than amongst the tribal peoples of West Africa. Peoples like the Dogon, in Mali, and the Fon and the Yoruba in Benin and Nigeria create exquisitely crafted and cared-for shrines. The Dagara of Burkina Faso are also great shrine builders.

In the Dagara tradition, shrine building is an indispensable part of any ritual. As in most African art, there is no separation between the artefact and what is being represented. As an African fetish is the god, or the spirit, or the soul it represents, so a shrine is a site of direct and unmediated access, and not a place of passive observation or distance. As a consequence, a Dagara shrine has that 'live' and immediate quality associated with African art. There is always an air of expectation around a Dagara shrine.

Malidoma Somé, whose name means "He-who-makes-friends-with-the-enemy", first came to the West in the nineteen nineties under orders from his village elders to bring their healing wisdom to bear on our damaged and damaging world. He immediately caught many people's attention with his erudition and his massive dignity. Joined by his wife, Sobonfu, Malidoma led a series of ritual retreats for men and women, offering us complex community rituals of rich creativity, heart-warming *communitas* and often life-changing profundity. Being a double PhD, he also gave us an intellectual framework for our ritualising and a whole cosmology, a spiritual map, behind what we were doing.

It was the Somés then who introduced me to the concept of 'live' shrines that informs and enhances the Dagara way. In Dagara cosmology there are five key elements: Earth, Fire, Water, Mineral and Nature, each, as in Chinese astrology, with its own birth-year. In any Dagara communal ritual, one can expect to see shrines set up to embody these five elements. They may serve as a base for Water people for instance, or for people born in a Nature year, or as a home for the energies and attributes associated with Fire (ancestors, passion, quickness, etc), Mineral (memory, stories, praise and warning), or Earth (nurture, home, level-headedness and comfort). Traditionally placed out of doors, and on the ground, such sites could consist of a simple mound of hand-sifted and smoothed soil, or a sunken bathtub, near a natural spring. They could also be astonishingly elaborate involving theatrical 'stage areas', proscenium arches, entrances, exits, fire pits and ceremonial pathways.

Over a couple of years I came to see that Dagara-style shrines can act like a kind of battery. They need care and attention in the making but once 'turned on' they hold some remarkably potent energies, so much so that they need attendant 'gatekeepers' to ensure safety and support. As a result of this they seem to provide extraordinary levels of healing, empowerment and life-changing insight, as will become clear in the next chapter.

~

Properly prepared shrines then, can have a profound effect upon us, and hold significant amounts of energy, however we choose to define it. Not so long ago I had a deeply moving experience, where the energy of a shrine, in this case a long-established medieval shrine, led to a profound outcome. All winter, I'd been over-working, travelling too much, and generally spending too much time in de-natured, glass and steel airports, hotels and conference centres. I was run-down, edgy and dehydrated, with a constant feeling of grit behind the eyes. In short, I was exhausted.

I'd also been wrestling with one of my occasional bouts of narcissistic inflation. Like many artistic people, I'm prone to swing between lacerating self-contempt and a kind of compensatory self-regard, or grandiosity. Not having spent the right kind of time with my mum when I was a baby, I grew up to become the kind of person who is constantly seeking the love and approval of others. There are millions of us with various degrees of this narcissistic disturbance, so many in fact that it's now a part of our modern way of living. Addiction and alienation on the one hand, and the media and celebrity culture on the other, have created a world in which narcissism is at the very heart of our cultural, organisational and political life. If, like me, you find yourself leading or speaking publicly on a regular basis, you tend to receive a lot of 'bigging up' which can inflate this wounded part of you. In my case, I'm particularly susceptible to compliments and need to closely monitor my reactions. Even so, every now and again, if I'm feeling lonely or tired, I can slip into the kind of grandiosity or arrogance that masks my lack of self worth. It's not pretty and I can usually get past it quickly enough – often by creating a small ritual, out in nature or under the stars, which gives me back my sense of human scale – but at its worst, it can make me insufferable or overbearing, to the point where I begin to hate myself, an ugly little cycle that serves no one.

I was therefore delighted to get a call from the Reverend Marie-Elsa Bragg, an old friend from Wild Dance workshop days who, having been ordained as an Anglican priest, was now working as a Chaplain at Westminster Abbey. We caught up and chatted ruefully about work and the need to take care of ourselves, at which point she offered me a private tour of the Abbey precinct. What I didn't grasp at the time was that I was stepping into a ritual – part vigil, part homecoming, part old-style mystery – for which I was to be profoundly grateful.

The afternoon began inauspiciously with pie and chips in a nearby cafeteria, a dash through mid-winter rain, and a security badge from a Dean's Yard office. I know the Abbey well enough, or parts of it, having spent many a Christmas Eve queuing so that I could sit in a kind of pagan communion with Auden, Hardy, Hughes and company in Poets Corner during the Midnight Eucharist, but Marie-Elsa is an accomplished guide and pointed out details behind the scenes, which made the building come alive for me.

Most importantly I felt a sense of the building as a national shrine. From the great West Door with its memories of royal weddings and state funerals, past the poppy-framed Tomb of the Unknown Warrior, you pass under the graceful vault of a nave that arches a hundred feet above you, and a hundred yards ahead. This adds to the sense of journey through time and space, so that by the time you walk around the Choir, and the Sanctuary, you have arrived at a place of resonant stillness. Everything leads to the Confessor's Chapel.

Imagine the Abbey as a figure laid out on the floor. If the West Door is the feet and the nave is the legs, the transepts are the arms and Henry VII's chapel is the head. This means that the heart of the building, the holy of holies, is the quiet, elevated chapel behind the richly-paved Sanctuary where the monarchs of England and latterly Britain have been crowned for nigh on a thousand years. It is this secret heart-space that houses the shrine of St Edward the Confessor.

This is the space that monarchs retire to, through a discreet door in the Altar screen, after they have been crowned in the Sanctuary. It was a place of vigil and contemplation for the warriors and princes who variously ascended to, or took, the throne of England. This horseshoe-shaped area, no more than thirty feet across, with a gothic screen at one end and a chantry at the other, was created by Henry III to house the remains of the Abbey's founder. Over the years it became a site of pilgrimage and healing. Despite attacks by iconoclasts and puritans, who smashed and destroyed what devotion had built, the tomb is still intact and the shrine remains.

King Edward the Confessor wasn't a priest and never took confessions. The title merely describes a kind of saint who was not a martyr. He was the last of the line of Alfred the Great, known far and wide as a holy man in his lifetime. After his death and burial in the Abbey, people were soon reporting miracles of healing around his grave.

And so I found myself, standing, unaccompanied, in a place I might never normally get to visit, let alone experience on my own. Marie-Elsa had discreetly left me, and I was standing in the small circle of Plantagenet tombs that surrounds the raised catafalque of the Confessor – defining one of the most exclusive mausoleums in the world – a silent gathering of the royal dead. To my left lay Henry III, in an elaborate gothic confection of porphyry and once-gilded wood. Next to him was Edward Longshanks, whose plain brutal block of marble spoke volumes about the 'hammer' of the Scots and oppressor of the Welsh. To my right Richard II was lying in effete and gilded splendour, while beyond him lay the effigy of Edward III, England's greatest warrior king; strangely wizard-like in his long flowing beard. Fifty years a king and over six hundred years dead, he lay poised and ready, still awaiting the call of some mythic horn. Beyond this ancient circle of kings and queens lay yet more sovereigns: Henry V the victor of Agincourt, mealy-mouthed Henry VII, poor young Edward VI, Bloody Mary and her glorious virgin sister Elizabeth I, Mary Queen of Scots and her son James I, Mary Stuart and William of Orange, and Queen Anne, the last of the Stuarts. Out in the echoing spaces of the Abbey, statesmen and prelates, poets and scientists gathered in death, a vast, imposing company, that spoke of towering achievement and lives well spent. A hundred feet above me the Abbey's gothic ceiling soared, while the sheer weight of history invested every inch of space around me with solemnity and gravitas. My self-regard and grandiosity began to ebb away.

Given the scale of its surroundings, the Confessor's Chapel is a remarkably intimate spot; not so much oppressive as welcoming and embracing, a kind of historical cocoon. The immense silence of the place, accentuated now and then by the muffled thud of a distant door shutting, or the echo of retreating footsteps, added to a growing sense of immanence, of almost tangible presence. As I stood there I remembered Malidoma Somé once saying that two of the most important attributes of a shrine were beauty and mystery. I bowed my head in acknowledgement of both.

Before she left, Marie-Elsa had shown me how kings and pilgrims would have knelt in the niches, placed their hands on circular indentations cut into the walls, and rested their foreheads against the skin-polished stone. I'm no churchman, and many years before I'd, rather foolishly, made a deal with myself never to bend the knee again, but I couldn't help but be curious about what it might feel like to kneel where so many had knelt before me, in a niche that has seen so much, and heard so many whispered entreaties. Looking around me in slight embarrassment, I knelt clumsily on the threshold of one particular niche, worn by countless thousands of knees. I placed my hands in the waiting roundels, and rested my head against the cool Cosmati stone. I breathed, relaxed and breathed again, letting out a long accepting sigh, and settled into the moment. I don't know how long I knelt there but at one point, the pilot in my head, the little observer who knows exactly what you're doing, even when you're utterly engrossed, became acutely aware of the extreme vulnerability of my stance. On my knees, arms out to the side and lifted up, hands pressed flat to the stone, and head resting limply, I saw I was in the archetypal position of surrender. In that moment I accepted my insignificance and, like untold thousands before me, I arrived, gave in and quietly began to weep.

I surrendered to the shrine and let its layered mystery hold me, support me, and heal me. Like a Dagara earth shrine, the Confessor's tomb 'earthed' me, drew out some of the cultural poison that occasionally re-infects us all, and re-instated a blessedly ordinary humanity. On the train home, I felt cleaner, and lighter, more solid and more whole.

Chapter Twelve

Living with Giants:
Archetypal Energies and Sacred Technologies

The purpose of ritual is to wake up
the old mind in us, to put it to work.
Z Budapest

L ife's not always serene and gentle. While smudging can purify and
calm us before a ritual, and a shrine can bring us to quiet tears, we
can also release immense and seemingly uncontrollable emotions
in liminal space. The gradual gentrification of western religion, with its
politeness and essential decency has, over the centuries, shut down and
denied many powerful human energies that have since found a home at
rock concerts, comedy stores, avant-garde theatres and football matches.
As the medieval mystery players and the Lords of Misrule understood only
too well, we need places for our rowdiness and our joy, our explosive anger
and our accumulated grief to be expressed.

It's also true to say that ritual itself is neither polite nor refined. There are
huge archetypal energies that can be unleashed in ritual space. Witness the
seething rage that we have seen erupt at funerals in the Middle East, or the
'mob-joy' expressed in the UK around royal weddings.

These energies, be they individual or communal, are an essential part of
our humanity. No matter how uncomfortable we may have become around
them, they are still going to arise. Anthropologists speak of ritual as being
able to contain the human shadow, to allow for spontaneous, dark, even
explosive behaviours. In the nineties, I became interested in finding a safe
ritual container that could hold these often scary energies, whilst providing
adequate means of expression.

One summer around that time I was studying the 'radical rituals' of the

Dagara people and working as part of the team that organised and supported the first communal rituals led in the UK by Malidoma and Sobonfu Somé, as I mentioned in the previous chapter. This became a deep dive into a whole new way of ritualising, during which I learned a great deal about these titanic energies, about their expression in liminal space, and about myself.

It is one of the great losses of our culture that three hundred years of slavery, colonialism, and cultural superiority have blinded us to the intricate yet down-to-earth genius of West African spirituality. The great spiritual traditions of the Fon, the Dogon and the Yoruba, and the philosophical subtleties of Ifa have, until recently, been grossly distorted and relegated to mere superstitions and mumbo-jumbo. Oddly this doesn't happen with other traditions. Buddhism, Hinduism, and Taoism, though often misinterpreted and misunderstood, are acknowledged as having great merit, while the spiritualities of America, Oceania and the Arctic have a kind of cool. Only African spirituality is still seen as dark and dangerous on the one hand, or superstitious claptrap on the other. This is ironic because it is these very cultures that have the surviving sacred technologies[36] to manage and process the supposedly dark and difficult feelings and behaviours that we in the West increasingly fear and deplore.

As any African child will tell you, a feeling is merely a feeling, and naturally expressed through the body. The trouble seems to be that we in the West are spending less and less time in our bodies and more and more time in our heads. This was the challenge facing the Somés as they sat in front of a roomful of predominantly nice, white, middle-class people one hot July evening on a wooded 'edge' in Gloucestershire, at the beginning of what was to become the first full-on West African grief ritual held in Britain.

Malidoma Somé had always considered Great Britain to be a particularly ghost-ridden island. He maintained that this was because Brits tended to shy away from open manifestations of grief. This left the dead un-mourned, when they needed to be fully grieved so that they might join the ancestors. As it stood, the lack of overt grief left them lost and abandoned, hence the numbers of wandering ghosts that cluttered our lives and psyches. Malidoma maintained that it needed the weight and power of communal grief to row the dead 'over to the ancestors'. Given the differences between a Dagara village and a group of British 'workshop junkies', a communal grief ritual in England was necessarily going to be a tall order. Malidoma began to consider how he might set one up and handed over much of the teaching to his young wife.

Sobonfu Somé appeared so young that at first glance it was quite hard for me to take her seriously, but she quickly proved to be as wise and as powerful as any teacher I had ever worked with. Thin, gawky, and angular with gap teeth and a smile that could melt the hardest of hearts, Sobonfu, whose name means "keeper of the rituals" was, like Malidoma, sent out into the world to pass on the wisdom of their Dagara elders. Having overcome her own loneliness and grief at the loss of her homeland, she quickly realised that there was a deep yearning in the West for some kind of connection, for community on the one hand and spirituality on the other. She set out to open doors in people's hearts, alongside the fiercely intelligent Malidoma, and over the coming years, was to lead us through some of the most powerful ritual experiences imaginable.

As far as the Dagara are concerned then, a grief ritual is aimed towards helping the dead to navigate their way over to the ancestors. The undoubted emotional or mental health benefits for the living are really a side issue, though no less useful or valuable 'in the village'. I began to see that, if the ritual came together, I would be serving my own un-grieved line of dead as much as, if not more than, myself. This was not going to be a neat therapeutic process.

Imagine an old Cotswold-stone country house, with a large lawn, a vast tulip tree to one side, and at its roots, a spring of the purest water. Imagine fields, with docile cattle, leading away to woods at either end, and opposite, a broad vista of the sleepy valley below and the hills of Gloucestershire beyond. This was to be the site of our first howling, snarling, and ultimately empowering West African grief ritual.

The Somés gave an introductory talk on the Dagara way of ritualising and the five elements of Dagara cosmology. It was announced that we would all be doing a non-specific *communal* ritual the following day, and that this would be a large and elaborate affair. The rest of the day was spent divided into five clans based on the Dagara elements. I was a general gofer for Sobonfu, who oversaw the practicalities, while Malidoma withdrew to prepare the area spiritually, and think through the implications of doing a grief ritual. With a hundred people industriously working away under her direction, Sobonfu had a great deal to do.

In true Dagara style, the ritual was to be housed in a 'village', an oval enclosure which was prepared at one end of the lawn. Within the oval was a semi-circle of element shrines, each built in the expectation that their function would become apparent as the ritual unfolded. The Earth Shrine held a large amount of soil from the fields that had to be sorted through for stones and then passed through a sieve, while the Fire Shrine involved a fire pit and a great pile of firewood that had to be collected from the adjacent woods. Each shrine was constructed using an immense amount of hard physical labour.

I learned a lot from Sobonfu about ritualising, but one thing stands out from that first day. I was on an errand for her and running toward one of the shrines when her voice cut across the countryside. "William. Stop!" I stopped. "Don't run," she said more quietly. "This is ritual space. You need to be respectful." I looked at her face and saw that she was absolutely serious. In Sobonfu's mind the ritual had already begun and the spirits were already present. My eagerness to serve had blinded me to the fact that I was working for her and that she felt responsible to the spirits. She expected a kind of impeccability from us when it came to our behaviour in liminal space.

At the end of the day, Malidoma and Sobonfu invoked the ancestral spirits and we were asked to connect with our ancestors, something that I found both stirring and surprisingly comforting as I imagined my ancestors running back through the ages, bringing a sense of continuation to my ragged and random life. We then rehearsed a chant that we would be using for the ritual. It was a simple invocation to the ancestors, going all the way back to the first grandfather and grandmother. This chant was to be sung for hours at a stretch, the following day, supported by a bank of *djembe* drummers who kept heroically to the same African rhythm.

In the morning Malidoma finally announced that we were about to start our full grief ritual. At the other end of the village from the element shrines there arose a huge semi-circular ancestral shrine. It was some twenty-five feet across and over ten feet high, made of greenery collected from the woods. A white sheet was spread on the floor in the centre and items people associated with their departed were spread among the greenery. The whole had a dark and sombre atmosphere, and was bounded at the front with a demarcating line of ash. This was there to separate us from the dead. Two 'gatekeepers' were assigned to either end of the line, their task being to stop any grief-distracted person from crossing the line between life and death, by throwing themselves towards the ancestors. Finally, at either end of the shrine, two fierce Dagara masks were mounted to further discourage the living from seeking to join the dead. Comfortable rural Gloucestershire was melting away around us.

While the group dispersed to search for meaningful oddments, or bits and pieces to add to personal 'grief-bundles' that would be put on the

Ancestors' Shrine, a group of us finalised preparations within the oval of the village. We set out rows of lanterns, made of nightlights set in earth-filled paper bags, to mark out the egg-shaped oval of the village. This now had the Ancestors' Shrine at the 'rounded' end and seating for five or six drummers at the 'pointy' end of the egg. Lastly we marked out a line that separated the village from the grieving space, which Malidoma more than once called the Road of Chaos. All was now ready.

At this point we all faced the Ancestors' Shrine and the 'ground rules' were laid out clearly so that there could be no misunderstandings and all would be kept safe. We advanced in a body towards the Ancestors' Shrine and cast our grief-bundles onto the white sheet in the middle of the shrine. We then returned to the village and lined up along the village boundary, which had become our starting line. The drummers took their places and the rest of us picked up the chant. The ritual began.

Initially, everyone 'stoked the fire' of the ritual by chanting and drumming, to serve others in their grief, but also to bring up their own by constant repetition. Then, when we felt the call to walk the Road of Chaos, we were to step forward and move directly toward the Ancestors' Shrine. At this point another member of the community was expected to follow us; not to comfort, but to watch out for us by standing a few feet behind us as we grieved, prepared to hold us back should we try to cross the line of ash. In the event of the supporter's grief being triggered by what was happening around them, they were to raise their hands and *two* other people would then come from the village, one to support the original 'griever' and the other to support the now grieving supporter.

It took a while, but soon men and women began to lose their inhibitions, crossing to the Ancestors' Shrine and giving way to years of pent-up grief, first in ones and twos, and then in their dozens as the ritual developed a momentum of its own. I remember escorting one woman back to the village after she had completed a particularly vocal and heartbreaking session of grieving. As we returned, like a pair of exhausted refugees, she looked up at me and said the most poignant thank you that I've ever received. We held on to each other like orphans in the storm, which in a sense is exactly what we were. We became friends after the ritual and well over a decade later she was still recalling it as a re-defining moment of communion and trust. To have someone watching over her, silently protecting her when she was expressing herself with such vulnerability, was a life-changing event for her.

Participants were now walking, staggering, sometimes even running towards the shrine. And suddenly Sobonfu seemed to be everywhere: chanting loudly in the middle of the front rank, instructing us how to keep an eye on the element shrines at the rear, checking to see if people were okay after coming back from the Ancestors' Shrine, pointing out to someone that they needed to support a griever as they broke from the ranks, shadowing another who had suddenly leapt forward in their grief, and calling for one of us to take over and then returning to the end of the line to help keep the chant going.

Suddenly I was overwhelmed by a wave of grief that swept me across the lawn and onto my knees before the Ancestors' Shrine. I howled uncontrollably, like a child, my mouth close to the ground, as wave after wave of feeling passed through me. And then I was shakily on my feet again, walking back, arm-in-arm with my smiling supporter, towards the line where I joined Sobonfu, who smiled encouragingly too, as we turned to stoke the fire of the chant once again.

After hours of chanting, drumming and grieving, the energy began to wind down, and we went indoors for a well-earned rest. In the dining room, over hot tea and biscuits, we congratulated ourselves on having shown Malidoma that we Brits really *could* express our grief. As it turned out, we'd hardly skimmed the surface.

In the morning Malidoma shocked us all by saying that there was a lot more grieving to be done and that we'd hardly begun. He wanted us to start the ritual all over again from the beginning. Grimly, we trudged out to the line and the drums kicked off their relentless African cross-rhythm, carrying the beat right into our bodies, quickly stoking the fire again to the point where people were returning to the Ancestors' Shrine as if there had been no break. We were diving deeper and deeper into our grief. In fact it seemed that the previous day had been no more than a rehearsal. A huge power seemed to be released as an archetypal quality entered the proceedings. The day crackled and blazed with feeling. As people returned from the Ancestors' Shrine they were clearly at another level of grief, wide eyed and distraught, their supporters now looking worried and out of their depth.

Quickly and forcefully, Sobonfu directed some of us back to the Earth Shrine and others to fetch water from the Water Shrine. She then guided returnees, some of whom had taken off their clothes and were clearly beside themselves, towards us, and instructed us to lay them on the ground where, as is the Dagara custom, they were liberally coated with cooling wet mud, mainly over the heart area, sometimes covering the whole body. This ancient grounding technique worked impressively on those who, moments before, had seemed utterly inconsolable and lost in their grief.

This went on for some hours as the day heated up and the ritual with it. At one point, having grieved at the Ancestors' Shrine more than once myself, and escorted numerous others to do their grieving too, I slipped into an altered state, flashing back to another time. In reality, I was sitting splay-legged on the muddy ground, with one of the boarding school survivors draped like a *pietà* across my lap. I was dazed and still brim-full of grief, though filled with compassion for this man who was covered from head to foot in mud and recovering slowly from his own profound experience before the Ancestors' Shrine. His unfocussed eyes stood out white in his muddy face, and I was minded of what veterans of war and trauma call the thousand-yard stare. Suddenly, following his gaze, I was looking out across a First World War battlefield, in which so many of our grandparents had fought and died. I shook my head and stared about me at this nightmare spectacle until another weird sight broke the bubble.

Out of nowhere, stepping down from the gravel drive towards the spring under the tulip tree, an elderly Englishwoman and a little boy no more than eight years old stooped to fill a bottle from the spring. Was she surprised to see a hundred-odd mud bespattered, naked crazies, howling and rolling around in a veritable mud-bath? Not a bit of it. The stiff upper lip was alive and well in Gloucestershire. As she gently but firmly led the boy back down the drive he looked back towards us, and beamed cheekily, just as a local child might in Africa.

Memories of my childhood came flooding back, and I became aware of how little the surviving old men of my village had actually spoken of their First World War experience. The old soldier's grief they held yet never expressed welled up in me. As soon as I saw that the man I'd been supporting was in good hands, I headed back to the Ancestors' Shrine one more time. I hit the deck, overwhelmed by an inconsolable sorrow that welled up from some echoing space deep within me. It was less raw and jagged than present grief but carried the immense weight of two generations' unwept tears.[37] It left me wracked but also cleansed, somehow even elated. Then I rejoined the line near Sobonfu and the ritual moved towards its natural end.

Malidoma carefully closed the ritual down. He chose two gravediggers who rolled up the sheet with its grief-bundles and took away 'the corpse' of our communal grief. In line with Dagara practice, they buried it, secretly, in a place that only they would remember.

That night I was deputed to guard the Ancestors' Shrine. Long after the deeply contented participants had gone to bed, I sat alone on the moonlit grass with the great shrine in front of me. I knew that I had witnessed something unprecedented, a full-scale grief ritual, unlike anything that had been done in Britain before, or rather unlike anything that had been done for many hundreds, perhaps thousands of years. I realised that I had touched what people were now calling the indigenous soul, the ancient atavistic part in us Westerners that knows the ancient ways of humanity. It felt like a prodigal's return.

~

In looking back on my first ritual with them, I was struck by how respectful the Somés were of the energies they were dealing with. There was no glee in what they were doing, no triumphal sense of 'getting a result', just a quiet satisfaction at having, by their lights, served the ancestral spirits of these islands. From where I sat they seemed to be working impeccably, creating safe ritual containers for whole communities to process *generations* of unexpressed grief.

On a personal level I had now been quietly purging my grief over a period of years, getting more and more comfortable with it, as I explored its causes, depths and parameters. I had also looked deeply into the fear that I had inherited from my mother, and on the way re-discovered the joy I had experienced as a child. What I had studiously avoided, what I had shunned and recoiled from, was the all-too-human rage I knew must be lurking within me. The Jungians I had come to know and respect had taught me that one can 'eat the shadow', by acknowledging, assimilating and re-absorbing our darker potentials, be that any kind of ugliness, as well as powers and talents. However, when it came to my anger I had tried all manner of workshops and therapies, to no particular avail. If my anger came up I just buried it again and pretended it wasn't there. It was another Dagara ritual that opened the door to my rage, a ritual more powerful than I ever could have imagined.

It happened the following year at a 're-birthing' ritual led by the Somés at the same venue. Once again I was a part of the team assisting Malidoma and Sobonfu, supporting Richard Olivier who was in the role of ritual stage-manager. I'd spent the better part of the day finding tools, helping to build a circular sequence of element and ancestor shrines that we were to process through later. I was tired, and I have to say, a little cranky. By the time the ritual started I was done in, but that was only the beginning of my troubles.

Community rituals can be long, drawn-out affairs. There are great pauses when queues before shrines grind to a halt while someone goes through an emotional process. Sometimes one of the shrines is *so* beautiful and *so* mysterious that every single participant stays just that little bit longer. Indigenous people are perfectly happy to get bored in ritual space, have a chat about the crops, or discuss the latest plan for getting water to the village, in the confident expectation that the ritual will end – well, when it ends. But in the West, we are used to *concentrating* on a properly timed experience that lasts no longer than a movie or a soccer match, all of which have clear start and finish times. We find it hard to accept that liminal space blurs all sense of time. Anyway, I was just cranky. I'm a fire person.

In his third book, on finding life purpose through nature, ritual and community, *The Healing Wisdom of Africa*, Malidoma describes the attributes of fire and the fire personality:

> *In the indigenous mind, fire kindles and sustains an animating and pervasive energy in all our lives... It is the mediator between worlds since it is very close to the purest form of energy. Any connection with ancestors, spirits and the Other World is mediated by fire ... A complete understanding of fire requires a serious relationship with death, and the dead. Because fire burns, those who relate to fire are often tense and must be clear about their intention in working with the fire. The tension referred to here is like a charge of energy about to burst. Those who carry such fiery energy are being prepared for energetic action that reflects, and is the result of, a touch from the other world.*[38]

By the time I had chanted eighty-odd people through the village, welcomed most of them back, and relieved all the shrine-keepers that needed relieving, I was exhausted. Student ritualist or not, I just wanted to wrap the thing up, secure the shrines, and get some well-deserved sleep. Richard came over and suggested that it was time for me to go through the process. By this time the rest of the team had gone through and only Richard and I remained. Rightly, he was reserving the last place for himself, and when I said I wanted to call it a day he said that Malidoma was specifically wanting – he may have said expecting – me to go through next. I bowed to the inevitable, and headed for the first port of call, the Ancestral Memory Shrine.

During our day of preparation, we had all been asked to consider our ancestors and to make an ancestor mask. I had determined that I was going to work around (or with/on?) a very specific ancestor of mine, a Jacobean bishop called John Overall, who was one of the church scholars who translated the King James Bible. The beauty of his clear and evocative language had stayed with me over the years, though I had never, until that day, connected him with ritual. I'd chosen him over an obviously mythical Viking of my East Anglian bloodline, because I wanted to explore the literary connection. Mask in hand, I plodded up to the Ancestral Memory Shrine and, as instructed by Malidoma, attached my mask of John Overall to one of the poles stretching up into the sky. He hung there amongst other masks, just another ancestor. I knelt and waited. Nothing happened. I stood. I looked up at the mask and thought, "Oh this is bollocks. It's just a paper plate, isn't it? I don't even know if I'm really connected to this man anyway." I shook my head like a tired bear, and disappointed, headed disconsolately over towards the Fire Shrine and its three pits of glowing coals, which we had dug out so laboriously that afternoon.

It was dark by now, and the Fire Shrine glowed red and threatening. I didn't know what time it was, and I can't remember much about stepping down into the trench, or standing between the shrine's surrounding fire pits, but I will never forget what happened next.

I need to say, as an aside, that I've always been overweight and, probably as a result of my childhood experience, have always had a really bad self-image. In fact I've always carried a great deal of shame around my body. I was the kind of man who never, ever took my shirt off in front of others, even on a beach. So there I was, standing between the fires, feeling wholly alone, and a little put upon, realising that the extraordinary heat of the fires was about to singe my army surplus fatigues if I didn't move on, when a wave of raw, animal energy blasted through me.

Once again, it was as if I was in another place and time, but this time in another body too. My muscles began to pulse as my blood surged around my veins, and I felt myself filled with an incandescent rage that rose from deep inside me, forcing its way out through my widening, growling, animal throat. My nice white middle-class anxieties had, in a red-raw moment, been ripped out of me. In every fibre of my body I was a bear, or more properly a *bear-sarker*, one of the bear-shirted ones, a wild Viking berserker. I was utterly invulnerable, and full of incandescent rage. My muscles seemed to bulk out, my hair stood on end, and my eyes burned in my head. I had short-circuited my bloodline and jammed my fingers in the socket of my Nordic ancestry. I was possessed. I began to roar. From the outside I imagine you will have seen a plump middle-aged Englishman standing in a trench between three fires, but on the inside I was undergoing an almost cellular sea-change. My breath rasped in my chest. My shoulders and back prickled as I felt myself swelling in bulk and in sheer, brutal strength. Abruptly, explosively, I ripped my shirt open, baring my chest to the fire, and roared out a killing defiance at the world. "*Odin!*" I bellowed from somewhere way, way back. "*Odin!*" The rage of it echoed down the valley and away into the night.

Dazed by this shattering of my metropolitan veneer, I looked through the flames to see Malidoma himself, crouched there where he had been waiting for me, eyes fire-lit and smiling but somehow understanding, nodding at the ferocious, bestial, yet infinitely more powerful creature I had become.

The rest of the re-birthing ritual passed relatively peacefully. The re-birthing itself, a powerful journey through a 'birthing hut' that recreates the muscular contractions of a birth canal, followed by a healing and loving welcome, left me exhausted and limp, more like a newborn pup than a human. At the Water Shrine I plunged myself deep under the surface, spraying a great arc of water as I came out gasping, but back in my own tired but tingling body. On the final walk back to the village I knew I had touched something profoundly mysterious. Through years of therapy and recovery, workshops and retreats, bodywork and alternative treatments, I had sought my 'lost power', whatever that was. And now I had met it head on. Furthermore, I had been gifted an insight into its terrifying human potential. For the first time in my life I really understood my shadow, and who I really was. I reeled at the knowledge, both inspired and scared.

Chapter Thirteen

Up On the Hill:
Bringing Ritual Home

Just as ecological theory explains how we are connected with all other forms of life, rituals allow us to recreate that unity in an explosive, non-abstract, gut level way. Rituals have the power to reset the terms of our universe until we find ourselves suddenly and truly 'at home'.

Margot Adler

M any of our modern problems come from our refusal to accept our original, less sophisticated, human natures. Nowadays, we tend to see ourselves as superior to the living world around us. This has caused us to withdraw from our essential interface with nature. In continuing to do this we have lost our sense of human scale, and with it our humility. Tragically, we have become hell-bent, inexorably dismantling the fragile eco-system that supports us. Whether this is a modern grandiosity, or an arrogance born of ancient fears, is hard to tell but the fact remains that we are divorced from the earth, and we are destroying it. This is far from rational. It is mad. No matter how much we like to think that we have got beyond our 'primitive' past, we clearly have deeply buried wounds that are beyond therapy, or analysis, or even language to heal. We are in trouble.

For some years the indigenous world has been sending ambassadors with news of a more practical way. Be it from Ecuador or Africa, the Amazon basin or the Arctic circle, shamans and medicine teachers have come to the West again and again, imploring us, as their 'younger brothers', to change. In the process they have tried to re-teach us a couple of basic and unavoidable truths: that the world is a single ecosphere and that we are a part of it. Sadly these generous people have been ignored or mocked. Worse, they have succumbed to our great Western "sickness" and been rendered ineffective, or ridiculous. Fortunately their rituals – at this point let's call them primal rather than sacred technologies – can heal us in places that years of talking are unable to reach. By enactment, by performing ritual, we can reconnect with something that lies at the very heart of our being human – our inseparable connection to the web of life.

I first came across this concept as a teenager, exploring the *Tao*, the paradoxical Chinese 'way that is not a way'. I found it hard to grasp though I instinctively folded it into my worldview where it lay dormant for about thirty years. Later, after I had discovered ritual, I was introduced to the groundbreaking work of Brian Bates, a professor of psychology who was running courses on Shamanic Consciousness at the University of Sussex. Back in the seventies, Brian had come across an Anglo-Saxon spell book in the British Library[39]. This led to a doctoral thesis, which in turn became a successful novel. *The Way of Wyrd*[40] describes the adventures of a young monk who becomes involved with a Saxon shaman, confounding both his faith and his view of the universe. What Brian re-discovered, through this young scribe, was the nature-based underpinning of Saxon, and Teutonic, spirituality – the *Web of Wyrd*.

Perhaps the best way to imagine the Web of Wyrd, as perceived by the ancient Anglo-Saxons, is to start with the idea of a vast tapestry, woven by the spinners of fate (the three Norns). Its fabric consists of the vertical warp, which is the strong thread of time. This is crossed by the softer, less hardy weft, which is constantly being added to, creating the unchangeable story of the past. The weft can change however. It is constantly expanding or morphing into new forms, and everything we do, and everything that is done, adds new layers to the ongoing tapestry. As a further consideration, we can add in the idea of the Web as a spider's web, in which every intersection and strand is interconnected, so that to tremble one part of the web is to effect a movement in the entire set of responsive, reverberating and resonant tissues.

Brian Bates' expanded modern thesis pointed me towards an altogether more fluid conception that incorporated ideas of mutual connectedness and relationship. Wyrd, for me, was clearly more than a narrow conception of fate. It became something akin to the Celt's *Awen*, the universal power behind life; or the Native American principal of *Wakan*, the Great Mystery permeating everything; or even the Hindu concept of *Brahman*, "the unchanging reality amidst and beyond the world".

To me the excitement lay in the fact that this newfound Wyrd didn't involve a religious dogma, but provided a connecting theory that spoke of these islands and had the equivalent depth of an Awen or a Brahman. More importantly it seamlessly mapped over the ancient Chinese concept of the Tao, the all-present, primordial essence, or fundamental nature of the universe, which I had been unable to grasp as a kid. I now realised that the Tao was not a way or a path, as I had tried to imagine it, but an underlying natural order of things. The Web of Wyrd, as re-imagined by Brian Bates, literally opened up the world to me. I had discovered a philosophical link, a foundation on which to build a ritual practice, and it felt like it might help me find a way back to the spontaneous, raw but exciting business of being fully human, a part of the world.

The last piece of the jigsaw was the landscape of Southern England, that gentle, motherly place of woods and pastures, that I'd fled to as a child, and later seen buried under motorways and housing estates. My love, for that's what it was, spoke of a need for devotion, if not worship, and pointed towards a deep and abiding connection.

The rituals I had been doing after reading Brian Bates, predicated as they were on a nature-based cosmology, were nudging me towards some kind of ritual work in the landscape. Meanwhile the deep, radical rituals I had been doing with the Somés had brought up recurring memories of my awed, hill-fort experience as a teenager in Dorset. It was comforting to think that I hadn't been crazy back then, but that momentary foretaste of a deeper reality had me yearning for another, more sustained glimpse. Through the big set-piece rituals of the last few years, I had done a lot of emotional work, and was much more comfortable in my skin. I felt I was ready to explore The Other, or The Invisibles, or the inner reaches of my psyche, or whatever was still calling me in that landscape. I was also coming to a crossroads in my life, and needed to make some important decisions. I started to think about doing a vision quest.

~

In many traditional cultures, a vision quest, alone in nature, is considered one of the best means of discovering one's life purpose, or of seeking spiritual guidance. From their teens on, individuals are encouraged to go out into the wilderness, with no food or water, in a kind of initiation, sacrificing all that it takes to live in the day-to-day world. Once there, they are expected to rely on strength of spirit to sustain them until such time as they might be granted a vision, or a dream. This may guide them for the rest of their lives. Some quest many times in their life, others only the once.

People have been heading off into nature to seek answers to their questions for millennia, though our knowledge of the form comes mainly from our understanding of the Native American version, what theLakota people call *Hamblecheyapi, Lamenting for a Dream*, in which the seeker, having prepared physically and spiritually, goes into the wilderness and stays there, without food or water, for up to four days, until they receive a vision of what the Great Mystery might have in store for them. It is often seen in the West as an initiation ceremony for youth, but it can be repeated throughout life and is ideal for anyone seeking access to spirituality or the imaginal realms.

Historically, the best known vision quest on record is that of Crazy Horse (or as his people would have called him *Spirited Horse*) who was a shaman as much as a warrior. It is said that before the Battle of the Greasy Grass, as the Battle of the Little Big Horn was known to the Lakota, Crazy Horse lamented for and received a vision in which he was told to do certain things that would guarantee victory against the white man and make him invulnerable in battle: to paint himself and his horse with a very specific war-paint, representing hail and lightning, and to wear a round stone with a hole worn in it. This gave him great *wakan*, great power, which enabled him to lead the Oglala and Cheyenne warriors into battle with confidence and a sense of invincibility.

Out-sitting is the Scandinavian version of the vision quest. The seekers prepare themselves and spend time alone in Nature in order to receive a message from The Other. This and similar Eurasian shamanic rites have variously included long walks in uninhabited tundra, fasting, sleep deprivation and being confined in a small area, marked out in a circle or underground. A Nordic out-sitting is invariably supervised by a shaman, often female, who sets the timeframe, arranges for the purification of the subject in a sweat lodge or 'pre-ritual', and organises what is in effect a debrief, or return, with a feast, or break-fast.

Back then in the nineties I had no real knowledge of what was required of anyone contemplating either a vision quest or an out-sitting, and I certainly couldn't afford to pay for a trip to one of the vision quest companies that were beginning to operate in the USA. So, from a conceited yet naïve place of half-learning – I didn't even think of asking a ritual elder to supervise or watch out for me – I decided to go down to my favourite hill in Dorset and simply 'sit out' in liminal space for a few days in the hope that I would be gifted a sense of what I needed to do. And if I should be gifted with a vision, or a dream, or a message from The Other, so much the better

The weather was good, and I got down to Dorset early. I had a small pack, with water and some emergency rations. By the time I had walked up the long straight climb of the Roman Road and arrived at the crest of the Hill, I had separated from the world enough to be nervous of what I was putting myself through. The sky was clear and blue and the sudden vastness of the view over West Dorset made me feel all the more cut off and lonely.

The Hill is a massive iron-age hill fort, second only to Maiden Castle, built over Neolithic beginnings, and wreathed in legends and ghost stories. Seen from the Dorchester-Bridport road it lies flat and huge on the northern horizon and, in those days, still had a single wind-sculpted thorn tree that sat in the middle of its flat surface like a button or a nipple. It also boasted a dark atmosphere and a reputation for ghostly happenings. There have been numerous (cider-induced) sightings of ghostly legions marching up the Roman Road. Being high up and exposed to the constant south-westerlies, it has never been a welcoming place and people tend to shun it by night. This suited me perfectly. Having walked around the ring of the uppermost grassy ramparts of the fort, I worked my way down a spur of land towards a limestone outcrop that jutted out over the pastured and wooded valley below. This was to be my spot, my solitary eyrie. I lay down my tarpaulin, sorted through my pack, and prepared to enter my ritual.

Day one was bad. I awoke to the tatters of a dream about my lost home and a wood, and a badger. I hadn't realised how uncomfortable my earth and stone bed was going to be and I was gnawingly hungry. I was also fractious, fidgety and distracted. I had wanted to develop a meditative practice but the Hill itself was a huge distraction. This vast and seemingly empty expanse of grassy upland was literally teeming with life. The sheep below and the buzzards that called out in front of my eyrie were not the only creatures dependent on the Hill for a livelihood; butterflies and insects of all sorts came out to sun themselves as the morning got underway, while a flock of finches chattered in a nearby thicket of hawthorns. Between the lonesome, *kee-ah, kee-ah* calling of the buzzards, the incessant chatter of the finches, and the sudden flit and flash of a small tortoiseshell or a marbled white butterfly, I was constantly being drawn out of myself. I was unable to settle into a meditative state, or calm my mind. By nine a.m. I was going stir-crazy, obsessing about the past and beating myself up about things I thought I'd dealt with years before. By ten I had given up and taken out the book that I had brought for the return journey home, a book on Taoism, which explored our relationship to "the ten thousand things", the myriad manifestations of the world around us. I wasn't connecting.

Acknowledging my difficulties with meditation, I had planned that I would allow myself a contemplative circuit of the hill, or a part of it, once a day – as long as I didn't engage in unnecessary activity (to conserve energy) and avoided all human contact.

By late afternoon I was going mad, feeling like a prisoner, even though part of me knew it was a trick of my 'butterfly mind'. I climbed around the hawthorns and down to the fields, where I found myself on the dismantled railway line that used to run down to the coast. I turned left and walked for perhaps a half a mile until I found myself below the old railway station. I heard snuffling beyond the hedge and peered through to see four young badgers eating bacon rinds on the lawn of the old rail-bed. I watched until the youngsters were joined by an older boar, who muscled in on their feast. I headed back towards my eyrie, relishing this delightful moment in a difficult day.

Day two was worse. My lack of preparation really began to tell as my obsessive thinking ran riot and I descended into a pit of blame and self-loathing. I felt trapped, cornered. My stomach was clenched and I was parched. At noon I threw in the towel and nibbled at some of my emergency rations. The water, tepid and tasting of my metal water bottle, was delicious. I decided that I would go down to the village and get a meal in the local pub that evening. The sole was mouthwateringly good but I knew I had been defeated in my ritual aim. In fact I had been routed.

On the way back to my tent, a badger burst out of the undergrowth and, completely ignoring me, fled across the road pursued by two others that caught him as he descended into the field opposite. A vicious little fight ensued with the three badgers becoming a cartoon ball of screaming, grunting, tearing aggression, until the first badger fled towards a distant hedge while the others followed nipping at his heels. I assumed this was an enemy from another set being repelled, though I later discovered that badgers can expel older boars for the sake of the clan. That night, back on my ledge above the valley, I burned some cedar incense on a charcoal briquette and asked the universe for a sign. In the night I heard strange snufflings in the darkness under the hawthorns and told myself that I was a fool for imagining spooks and ghosties.

The following morning, I awoke at first light and ritually greeted the sunrise, which seemed to warm and relax me. I finally, formally, acknowledged my pent-up, neurotic foolishness and gave myself over to the Hill and whatever it might bring for the rest of my stay. At last, I took off my watch.

Over the next two days, having so signally failed, I simply sank down into myself. It was as if all the resistance in me had floated away and left me with nothing but myself, and the silence. Yet it was a very different 'myself' to the wild-eyed, worried creature who had arrived two days earlier, and the silence wasn't really a silence at all. It was a vast yet intimate conversation that seemed to surround me. What had started out as a self-imposed, egocentric ordeal turned into a deep experience of the Hill; with days spent looking, listening and becoming aware of things that seemed somehow, in their different ways, to want to engage me too.

Something happens when you start to pay attention, really pay attention, by which I mean soften your focus to take in the myriad things that we usually ignore by being so singly, so inexorably focused. Things that I had never spotted before seemed to tumble into my awareness: a soft grey thrush's feather resting on a leaf; a small blue-brown butterfly warming itself on a stone; two crows in the distance, mobbing a hawk in the high blue air. I gradually re-discovered the effortless attention of the young boy I had once been; the kid who seemed to notice everything, to mark it and file it away, like Kipling's "Little-Friend-of-all-the-World" in the famous game in *Kim*.

I became very quiet, like an animal, not through fear but by simply belonging. Late in the afternoon of the third day I climbed down from my rock, walked along the rail-bed and turned left up a lane with a hedge on one side and a narrow grass verge on the other. At the end of the lane lay a field of ripening barley, stooped heads whispering in the breeze. As I walked by this field I became aware of an odd sound that came from the barley-stalks and seemed to keep pace with me. At first I couldn't make any sense of it, and then I realised that I had heard it before, on the lawn at the old railway station, and under the hawthorns on the Hill. It was the sound of a badger muttering to itself as it moved along, a complicated trill of extended announcements including a whole spectrum of wittering, chittering, and chirruping sounds.

I spoke to it, gently repeating its mutterings as best I could. There was a silence, during which I expected the badger to flee or burst out of the barley and cross back to the hedge. Instead it repeated a short riff of chittering noises, which I returned. We both moved on, repeating the process, exchanging witterings and counter-witterings for some minutes until I ran out of repertoire or the badger realised that I was no conversationalist. There was a rustling and a ripple through the barley as my acquaintance moved off in a different direction.

Over the next hours and days I kept settling, ever more deeply, into the landscape: a small herd of deer, seeing me in plain sight, calmly moved off at an angle across a field; a tawny owl hooted to me as I passed by on my way 'home' from my evening meal at the pub; a big buzzard came up to the very lip of the rampart where I was sitting, her yellow eye checking me out, so close that I could almost reach out and touch her. And again and again, there were the badgers.

The First Nation people of America say that on a vision quest you are likely to meet your totem animal, your guardian spirit from the animal world, or world of spirit (indigenous peoples tend not to make the distinction). They also say that if you see an animal more than four times, it's trying to tell you something. Without going into every encounter, over four days, in threes and fours, and on their own, I saw twenty badgers. Accepting that I might have seen some more than once, I still saw more of these secretive creatures on this visit than in my entire life, and I grew up in badger country! Even if I didn't quite buy the 'spirit-animals-trying-to-get-in-touch' idea I was intrigued enough to worry the metaphor; to think through the experience like a Zen koan, an insoluble puzzle that gets you through to the next challenge. In the absence of a vision, and I had surely blown that one, what could twenty badgers possibly have to tell me about my life?

On the afternoon of my last day I made a final circumambulation of the Hill. As I walked along the grassy rail-bed, I was confronted by yet another badger, this one dead and pulled to pieces by foxes and buzzards. His yellow-white skull and worn-down teeth suggested that he had died of old age. I took this skull as a gift, a true souvenir, and he sits in my study to this day, his jawbone solidly attached to his skull, unable to let go. For this was the message that my vision quest gave me, that I should hold on like a badger, hold on no matter what. The badger family are unique in the animal world, in that their jaws are attached to their skulls – they cannot be disarticulated. This of course was their downfall, in that, when pitted against bull-dogs, they literally couldn't let go once they had bitten back. Because of this badgers were thrown into pits with 'sporting' dogs for hundreds of years. The badgers told me that I should never give up, and never go back to the 'easy' life of the casinos. In the months ahead I took their advice. My life began to pick up momentum.

Above and behind and around this message, like *Wakan Tanka* or the *Wyrd* itself, there lay a deeper truth. When we shed our busy selves, when we slow and pay attention, the ten thousand things can approach us, and meet us. The walls we build up with our worries and our obsessions, our ambition and our drive, can fall away and we can be seen as well as see.

On my last night in Dorset I *think* I had a dream. I was standing below my old eyrie. It was night time and a harvest moon was cresting the ash trees. There was a badger in front of me, an old boar, close to death, alone in a field of stubble. He was perfectly still and quite unworried; I knew he was unworried. Slowly, like a wolf raising his head to howl, he lifted his snout to the cool night air. But there was no sound. He just hung there, relaxed, his whole body curved and pointing to the sky. As I watched him, I smelled the scents that he was smelling, and my dim eyes saw the glow of the moon. I heard a rustling in the trees as a pheasant settled, felt the invisible movement of deer on the Hill. Like the badger, for a moment, I raised my head, and I was a part of everything.

Chapter Fourteen

The Bardic Role:
Public Ritual at Work and in the Community

Ritual is a way of structuring time so that we, not employers,
the market, or the media, are in control. Life needs its pauses,
its chapter breaks, if the soul is to have space to breathe.
Jonathan Sacks

Paulette Randall has been a friend since early theatre days. She's a powerful woman and a multi-talented theatre practitioner with an instinctive understanding of the edge between performance and sacrament. A few years ago, out of work and trusting to fate, she was sitting in her flat when the phone rang. It was Danny Boyle, the film director who had worked with her years before at the Royal Court Theatre. He asked her to join him in devising and preparing the opening ceremony of the 2012 London Olympics.

You don't say no to a call like that. What followed was a whirlwind of pressure and activity that called on all her talents as a director, writer, producer – and traffic controller – with everything accomplished under a blaze of suspicious scrutiny and the common belief that the whole thing would be a disaster. The end result was a triumph for Boyle and his team, and Paulette was hailed for its multicultural flavour and reach. This was as much due to their instinctive adherence to the unwritten rules of ritual – holding intention, allowing for the spontaneous, and paying attention to the detail – as it was to the £27 million budget or the tens of thousands of volunteers, athletes and audience members there on the night. They stepped back from the ever-growing pomp and grandeur of the last few Olympiads and created a magical narrative structure that held viewers spellbound and provided the stadium audience with moments of true ritual, keeping to an essential human scale that had been lost in previous opening ceremonies.

While the team's approach was very much one of storytelling, led by screenwriter Frank Cottrell Boyce, there seems to have been an understanding that the whole thing was a ritual too, leading to an official opening and the symbolic lighting of the Olympic flame. In London this involved the solemn lighting of Thomas Heatherwick's extraordinary Olympic cauldron which Boyle had insisted be sited within the stadium, rather than high up, competing with the bloated offerings of earlier Olympiads. The cauldron's constituent parts were effectively smuggled into the arena by the athletes, in plain sight, then 'reconstituted' as a vast, lotus-like copper flower. It was then lit, by young nominee athletes, at which point it rose into the air and became a cauldron of fire. This was a genuine *coup de théâtre*, a shaman's trick if you like, but the effect was a moment of true ritual, and awe, held globally and witnessed by an estimated *nine hundred million* viewers.

It might seem mad to imagine that a vast outside broadcast event involving 10,000 volunteers, as many athletes, and millions of viewers, might be a ritual, but that was the case. During the proceedings there were moments when things shifted, within the bowl of the stadium itself, into true spontaneous ritual. For instance, during the *Pandemonium* section showing the growth of the Industrial Revolution, there was a minute's silence – risky enough at any open-air event but doubly so during a five and a half hour epic like the opening ceremony – to commemorate the dead of two World Wars. As pictures of tommies, poppies, and the names of a decimated First World War regiment were shown on the stadium's screens, people instinctively rose to their feet in silent respect, a visible and spontaneous manifestation of *communitas*.

This honouring of the dead may have been a link to the very first Olympics held some two thousand seven hundred years earlier. Some believe that the first Olympics were held to honour and acknowledge death. Experts cite Homer's *Iliad*, which has Achilles holding funerary games in honour of his dead friend Patroclus.[41] In a time of ceaseless warfare and reduced life-spans, mock battles and competitions would have provided a sense of ritualised control over death and grief. Perhaps in future games – in a contemporary world where ugly little wars, internecine strife and climate-related disasters increasingly abound – we could make this clearly present yet unacknowledged aspect of any Olympiad more conscious.

Afterwards, I spoke to Paulette about her experience of the evening itself, and was curious if she had experienced any moments of true ritual. When did the hair on the back of *her* neck stand on end? "It happened twice," she said. "Once during *The Green and Pleasant Land* sequence, just before the televised transmission. I looked around and everyone was in character: shepherds, villagers, cricketers. I mean *everyone,* hundreds of them. Because of all the secrecy, we hadn't even managed a full run through, but they were just so *in it.* It was magical. And then again at the forging of the rings."

As she spoke I remembered the insistent pulsing music at the coming of Pandemonium, with seven great chimneys astonishingly rising from the ground, and Kenneth Branagh as Isambard Kingdom Brunel beaming approval as the Industrial Revolution overwhelmed and dismantled old Britain, ushering in Blake's dark satanic mills. With Dame Evelyn Glennie looking wild and mysterious, and a thousand volunteer drummers beating upturned bins and buckets, the intensity built and built as four huge rings were flown in on wires and a stream of simulated metal ran down a winding channel to be cast in a great circle, to be beaten by innumerable ironsmiths until it was lifted up to become the linking centre of the five glowing Olympic rings.

Clearly something more than a simple piece of storytelling had occurred. Twenty-six million Britons and hundreds of millions from elsewhere had, understanding it or not, been involved and engaged witnesses to a genuine ritual around the transformation of a nation. In the morning the press were ecstatic in their reviews. The ceremony seemed to have given permission for people to think differently about their country, to shake off their tired irony and cynicism and to accept themselves and their new identity.

Much good ritual depends on a narrative, either a mythic journey or a wonder tale with its fanciful windings and meanderings. This had been a slow beating out of a ceremonial narrative that, in its care and loving attention to detail, helped us all to see ourselves differently. Add in the odd superstar and an eighty-six year old monarch seemingly jumping out of an aeroplane, and you have enough to take you right out there, challenge your perceptions, and bring you back home again, leaving you somehow changed. That's more than an empty ceremony, that's a radical ritual.

We don't have to buy the idea of vast global rituals as a regular occurrence, but the possibility of meaningful secular ceremony on a grand scale *is* there, as the opening of the XXX Olympiad proves. There is a potential for good here and the possibility of a whole new ceremonial form that incorporates deeper aspects of ritual. We have only to hold a ritual intention and keep the technology within bounds, and the *communitas* to be found in true rites could be ours more commonly. By creating large-scale rituals that serve, rather than control, we can create genuine fellowship and breathe new energy into worn-out old forms, as well as developing understanding across frontiers and bridging the ever-deepening divisions of class, religion and wealth that plague our damaged world.

~

Public rituals, be they massive in scale like the Olympics' opening ceremony, or more intimate affairs like weddings or funerals, call for a different energy than anything one might summon up when working with an individual. There's a necessary theatricality to the proceedings and a far more performative edge to any storytelling, direction or movement that might be involved. As a poet and sometime theatre professional, I had always been interested in the presentation skills of my various teachers, but I gradually became aware of another essential aspect to their work, which people call 'holding'. Holding in this context is a vague, indefinable word that seems to imply an intimacy that often isn't there. I imagine it comes from the concept of holding people in one's regard and in a sense, that's all it is. I've heard practitioners denigrate holding as a new age myth, and others swear by it as a vital part of their working practice. Therapists seem to like the word, as do some performers, but there's not much professional agreement about what it might actually entail.

So what is it? One of the education practitioners at Shakespeare's Globe once watched me working with a group. "I can see what you're doing." he said. "It's like you're throwing out a psychic envelope and keeping people in a bubble of your attention."

This is all quite arcane, of course, but it's not entirely fanciful. Another Globe practitioner at that time, Master of Voice, Stewart Pearce, once told me the story of his meeting with the great soul diva, Tina Turner, who at the time was filling vast stadia around the world. Stewart had found himself backstage at Wembley Stadium, watching spellbound as she held tens of thousands of people enthralled, seemingly having a direct connection with every one of them. Finding her both down to earth and approachable, he asked her how she did it. "How do you hold all those people like that?"

She told him she used to stand behind the curtain at the back of the stage, peering through a chink at her audience. As they streamed down the aisles and made their customary rush for the stage, she would stand there, watching them, repeating, over and over, the simple phrase "I love you... I love you... I love you... I love you..."

And that's it. That's what 'holding' is all about. A kind of cross between *darshan* or blessing on the one hand and *agape* or *caritas* (the non-sexual love we used to call 'charity') on the other – a state of wholly loving attention.

I once spent some time in the company of Archbishop Rowan Williams, who came to stay with us when giving a poetry reading for our *On the Border* poetry series in Wales. His capacity for holding, lovingly holding, individuals and groups in his benign attention was both awe-inspiring and humbling to watch. Everyone who stood before him got an equal blast of full-on, wholly instinctive love. At the time he was suffering the grossest assaults and betrayals around his leadership, and yet anyone who spoke to him was bathed, or rather held, in his love. This was holding of the purest kind; selfless, authentic and ultimately in service to both his people, and his God.

Now there's a vast spectrum between an Archbishop of Canterbury at one end and a gyrating rock star at the other and yet, in these instances at least, they seem to be coming from the same attentive place and employing the same skills and attributes. These are the very capabilities called for if we are to hold and create our own public ceremonies and turn them into meaningful rituals. Whether in rehab or public memorials, remembrance events, or initiations, we are going to have to consider terms like holding, debriefing, and ceremonial narrative, just as much as authenticity and intuition.

This necessarily calls for a particular kind of person and points towards a role in the modern world that was historically taken up by priests and shamans, poets and bards. A role in which people of *character and sensitivity* step into public life more fully, 'speaking for us all' in times of ferment and social change. I believe this role to be still valid, perhaps essential in the modern world if we are not to be 'homogenised' and de-humanised by the global economy, or overwhelmed by the irreversible changes that are seemingly in store for us. It is a role for the activist, the artist and the healer in us all. I call it the Bardic Role.

Towards the end of the nineties, I had been exploring the Bardic Role in rehab, working with ritual and poetry to help sensitive and wounded people reconnect with themselves, and the wider world that they had somehow shunned or avoided. I had been able to develop my holding and attending capacities and was now thinking about broader 'performative' issues of presence, and visibility.

At about this time I was invited to work with Richard Olivier, who had moved on from personal development to working in organisations with leaders. I hummed and harrumphed as many artists do about working in the corporate sector (which it appeared was no friend of the things I held dear) but then I read a book by the poet David Whyte called *The Heart Aroused: Poetry and the Preservation of Soul in Corporate America*.[42] David's groundbreaking 'soul work' in organisations convinced me that there was good work to be done and issues to be addressed. I sensed that organisational life was a place to delve into the Bardic Role more fully.

~

There's a feisty little book by Daniel Prokop called *Leaving Neverland: Why Little Boys Shouldn't Run Big Corporations*.[43] Underneath the broad comedy, Prokop makes a devastating point. That many of the ills of the corporate world – the bank collapses and the oil spills, the unconscionable lack of social responsibility and the wholesale pillage of potentially wealthy populations – stems from the simple fact that men (still mainly men) in Western cultures are no longer initiated. This means that we are often led at work, and in our politics, by immature, needy, narcissistic and just plain unreliable *boys*, who are disinclined to deal with their own mess, let alone the mess of the corporations and political entities they lead.

The more I worked in the corporate field, the more men like this I came across. Clever, ambitious and well trained, but, when you scratched the surface, unsure of themselves and full of doubt; inheritors of what academics have called the "Imposter Syndrome" which repeats the eternal refrain "I've been lucky. I shouldn't be doing this job. It's just a matter of time until I'm found out."

I remember speaking to the urbane and hugely experienced chairman of a global communications giant at a seminar I was delivering. This immaculately turned out 'merchant prince', who exuded confidence and urbanity, confided that the issue over which he lost most sleep was that of succession. "To be frank, I don't see the right calibre of people coming up. We can't find the men and women we need to run the concerns we have created. It's as if something were missing."

This was where our experience in ritual became most useful. Developing longer, two, three and five-day retreats, Richard, Nicholas Janni and I began to offer delegates small 'breakthrough sessions', ritualised group 'processes' in which executives confronted inner voices, or other damaging issues, and had an opportunity to re-imagine and re-experience themselves at an identity level within the safe container of ritual space. We didn't need too much ceremonial or paraphernalia; with just the odd white sheet or a single candle, we found that we were holding true initiations. At their best these rituals had the feel of genuine rites of passage. The away-day corporate venues provided a sense of (often international) separation; the ritual a legitimate transition, and the closing sessions a powerful sense of homecoming. People reported life-changing experiences and shifts.

Occasionally we would touch the face of The Other, by which I mean that something extraordinary would happen that transcended our small group experience and shone a soulful light upon us all. One such occurrence happened when I was working with an organisation in Germany. Fred was a senior executive for a major global extraction giant. He was a quiet, clean-cut and thoroughly decent man, yet one who had a problem. Every time he was asked to speak about his subject (safety and reducing fatalities in a business notoriously wasteful of human life) he choked, and had to stop. He was filled with grief and was literally unable to continue. This had affected his promotion prospects and left him something of a laughing stock amongst the senior leadership, in spite of his experience, history and expertise.

We worked in the small groups, and his story came out. A dozen or more years before, he had been woken in the middle of the night and flown down to an opencast site in Africa where he had spent five days under fire, pinned down by rebel guerrillas while he had tried to get nine dead colleagues out of the wreckage of a plane that had been brought down, caught in the crossfire of the conflict. When he returned to headquarters he was told to take the rest of the day off and be back at work the following day. Being a good corporate soldier he had done just that, and shut it all in, not even talking to his wife and family from whom he became increasingly estranged. By the time we met in Germany, he and his wife were at the point of splitting up.

As Fred spoke to the group, the grief of years spilled out, and a ritual seemed to form itself around him. I pointed out that he seemed stuck in his own version of the Underworld. He used the word 'Hell', so, seeing him alone and fearful like Dante in his *Inferno*, I asked another member of the group to take the role of his Virgil, his guide and supporter.[44] We next made a path from a pile of black towels that happened to be in the room. I asked Fred and his guide to stand at the midpoint. At one end of the path we piled up all the furniture in the room, recreating the air crash, and in it we placed two members of the group, representing those who died in the crash. At the other end I placed the women in the group, who were there to represent his family and home.

Fred's task, his rite of passage if you like, was to say what he needed to say to the dead, whom he had been carrying around with him for twelve years. On hearing these instructions, Fred howled and had to be comforted by his Virgil. They stood there for a while as I briefed 'the dead' on what to say when he addressed them. Eventually Fred looked up and, through his tears, told them how sorry he was to have failed them (as if he could have done anything from thousands of miles away). As he stood there the victims of the crash spoke with all the authority of the 'towering dead'. "It wasn't your fault, Fred … It wasn't your fault."

The effect was electric. Fred smiled, hugged his Virgil and stood upright for the first time since I had met him. It was a major shift, but his journey through the Underworld wasn't finished yet. I turned him round at this point and asked him to tell his story as succinctly as possible to his 'family' at the other end of the path. As he spoke we made a rope of tablecloths and towels and tied it around his waist, giving the other end to 'the family' and instructing them to pull him home as and when they really felt his story touching their hearts. At this point we were all in tears, watching Fred as he opened his heart and was pulled home, where he was welcomed like the long lost, but beloved, wanderer that he was.

Such moments are not as rare as we might think and for every Fred (who was reconciled with his wife and later promoted to Vice President in his firm) there are others who undergo similar, if less overtly dramatic, transformations in an organisational context. For the sake of corporate sensibilities we may call it 'impact coaching' or 'symbolic action' but the fact is that for the most part we – I and other practitioners like me – are creating rituals in all but name. The more of this work that gets done, the better the standard of leadership, and we certainly need good leaders.

With a couple of old friends who are familiar with both the work and our need for 'corporate ritual' I have long harboured the fantasy that we could create a full rites of passage programme for executives; meeting the requirements of any 'merchant prince' and developing, over time, a cadre of initiated, trustworthy and fundamentally *solid* leaders-in-waiting. Is this just pie in the sky? I'm not so sure. I've seen things change over the fifteen years or more that I've been working in organisations and I'm encouraged by the changes in attitude that I have seen. Today people like me are proven suppliers with a respected track record. I have even helped to lead overnight initiations for one global corporation.

~

Of all public ceremonies, the most agreeable to hold are weddings. When considering marriage in a non-religious setting, some look to be witnessed or welcomed as a couple into the community, others seek an experience that speaks to their particular, often non-religious, spirituality. So, when creating a wedding it is important to tease out and honour the inner lives of the couple: the artistic, cultural, or spiritual ideas of both parties, even if they are not fully formed. This is not so much in order to 'get it right', as to allow for The Other, or their version of The Other, to enter into the proceedings.

Perhaps my most complex, demanding and, from my point of view, satisfying wedding was that of my friends Pam and Pete whose wedding came about by chance and circumstance. Pam had recently been diagnosed with a life-threatening, possibly terminal, illness. Moments like this can really bring couples together and they were no exception. Pam sets the scene:

> So after 14 years, the time came for us to marry. After all the times together and apart, the bliss and the arguments, turning our backs on each other and our fronts to each other, we finally turned in, to face each other. Pete asked me just as I was on the point of asking him and I said yes, immediately, before doubt had flickered anywhere.
>
> It was, of course, clear that we wouldn't want anything "usual" and asked good friends William and Juliet to be our celebrants. We didn't know what this would mean, or at least I didn't. I'd never been married before and wondered how far we could pull at the collective possibilities of ritual and celebration and it still be a wedding.

Having agreed to celebrate the wedding, Juliet and I were faced with a daunting task – to create a ceremony that could hold, if necessary, a huge amount of feeling, concern, and very possibly fear. As for the couple themselves, they were being brave, but sounding fraught, in that dreadful place of unknowing. I had the germ of an idea, of a wedding that would hit the spots of witnessing and community while tapping into deeper reserves of support. Pam again:

William and Juliet came over for a lush day of wild planning. They made suggestions to see what held our interest, alighting on a Northern European ritual, a hand-fasting to literally tie the knot. Yes! This way everyone at the wedding would be actively involved. We decided that a smaller inner group of close friends would open and hold the ritual space, softly inviting others (another 50, as it turned out), less familiar with live ritual, into a well-prepared space.

What actually emerged was a two and a half day, rolling ritual that involved West African, contemporary British, and Native American ritual components, supported by a spine of Northern, that is to say, Anglo-Saxon and Norse ceremony. A series of deepening rites eventually focussed everything towards a light-hearted and gentle hand-fasting which involved everyone in the community tying the loving couple together with ribbons and strips of cloth.

I needed to be in safe hands – for me, Pete and the process, to be cradled in the palm of a hand that would both curl in and then lay out flat.

What is rarely discussed in these kinds of rituals is the depth and care that goes into the preparation of ritual journeys. We arranged everything – from the first meeting at the registry office, to the final sweep up and ritual shut down. We designed a full set of rituals including: a ritual welcome and smudging of the core team and a circle of commitment; a decoy ritual to combat any latent negativity around the couple; a West African back-to-back session for the couple, which had them asking the sorts of questions of each other that we all should ask before we wed. What do you hope for, or yearn for, or fear in this relationship?

And the intensity of a space that took us, alone with William and Juliet, down into the murk and possibility of what this relationship has been, and could be for the future. We got to acknowledge and name and move on ready for the wedding. We got to clear the decks and take a fresh breath.

We trooped out after dark to burn our bundles on the Viking-style pyre of negativity, then changed for dinner, which featured a good old fashioned bragging session about either the bride or the groom in honour of the Norse god Braggi, the father of the brag!

After dinner we entered into the Groom's Ordeal, another West African Wedding ritual in which the groom and his friends gather to 'sell' the groom to the bride's supporters by extolling his virtues and skills. The bride's friends meanwhile are there to see that she doesn't swoon away at the groom's beauty or get swept away by his friends' salesmanship. A great deal of fun was had, and wonder expressed, as the men performed a flawless song and dance routine. Finally the groom stepped forward and made his own pitch. Everyone was agog as he spontaneously stripped everything down to the bare essentials of his deep respect and profound love for his beloved.

The morning of the wedding itself began with an optional greeting of the dawn by half a dozen brave souls, who enriched the process by honouring the morning and the landscape that was welcoming and supporting the event. This was followed by the beautifying of the ritual space, a lovely room with a cupola at the centre of its domed ceiling. The guests were smudged on arrival and all awaited the bride and groom. Pam again:

Everyone cheered Pete as he walked into the "hilarium" space (at last!) and everyone sang to me as I entered.

They surely did – a smooth and gentle, lullaby-like song, that carried Pam towards her man. The deeper ritual work of the previous day had done its job. Everyone was relaxed and easy, "unceremonious" as a smiling guest said later. In fact the anxieties and awkwardness that may have surfaced had been contained and managed, burned up, spoken out loud or laughed off, the day before.

The ceremony of the hand-fasting itself was a friendly, relaxed, communal affair. We gathered in an informal circle around the bride and groom to see them wed. There were vows, and poetry, and the knot was tied, with old and young, as always, vying for who would tie the couple's hands together first. That night there was a feast, and a *Ceilidh*, with clowning, poems, songs and music.

In the morning there was yet another ritual as the core group gathered to offer tiny yet meaningful presents, all of which were packed into a hand carved, antique dowry-box into which I finally placed the wrapped-up and bound knot of the hand-fasting.

Finally, we cleaned up and returned things to nature before the core group met for one last time, speaking their heartfelt farewells in the sacred space where the hand-fasting had been held. Many of them had experienced something deeper than they had expected, but all of us had done something important together, regardless of our various belief systems, religions and spiritualities. Driving home to Wales, Juliet and I strayed off the beaten track getting progressively lost. Eventually, by a wood near the border, we stopped so that we could return the unused ritual paraphernalia, chocolate, oat flour and cloths to nature, offering our thanks for a successful ceremony. As we got back in the car Juliet paused, turned to me, as tired and satisfied as I was, and acknowledged our friends' journeys from ambivalence to a solid and loving marriage. "Well they're well and truly married now," she said, and got in the car.

Chapter Fifteen

Re-enchanting the Forest

Let the heart be at peace. Observe the workings of creation.
Absorbed in the wonder of the Way you can cope with whatever comes.
When death comes you are ready.
Tao Te Ching

The Wanderer seeks to put his ego in a double bind, a checkmate
that makes it impossible to continue the old story.
Bill Plotkin

As I sit here in Maine, looking out at Albion Pond, this perfectly unremarkable New England pond, which I have come to love so very much, I am struck by an almost overwhelming wave of gratitude. It's not just the beauty of the pale sun burning off the morning mist, nor the sight of Juliet, pottering about in her happy, holiday way. It's not even the sudden presentiment I have that the female bald eagle is about to make her high-pitched whistling cry and swoop out of the pines before vanishing into the morning. It's a slow dawning that wells up from deep within me, a recognition that I have come full circle and re-found the boundless connection of my boyhood. Without even thinking about it I have stumbled back into the garden of belonging that I lost all those years ago.

This is not so much an epiphany as a quiet acknowledgment, a gentle nod towards the reality of my randomly sown and slow-growing way of being. Spending time with the W'abanaki has shown me that my worldview and theirs have a great deal in common. Their matter of fact yet lived relationship with the world around them has helped me to see that my evolving 'way', such as it is, has brought me to a place of genuine quietude. I still have bad days and periodically lose it – as Tom Pesko might say, the sickness still gets me – but my deep sense of having a place in the world, even when I have no place of ancestral belonging, is unshakeable. I am a fully paid up member of what the great New England poet, Mary Oliver calls "the family of things" – and I am truly thankful.

~

In many ways I, and the people of my ageing generation, have been lucky. Having had the leisure to explore our potential, many of us have discovered ways to bring meaning back into our own and other people's lives. Without losing our modernity, through therapy, recovery, meditation, and, in my case, through ritual, we have to a degree found healing and fulfilment. In doing so, we have reconnected with others and crucially with the environment.

By putting ourselves in proximity to nature and actually addressing it, we engage. In engaging we begin to feel a kinship, and at that point we begin to re-consecrate what we are addressing. The planet and its denizens are made holy again. This *feeling* aspect is crucial in ritual. It bypasses all the books on deep ecology, all the seminars on environmental collapse and all the scary documentaries on extinctions. Once we *feel,* we create relationship and in relationship we become truly human again. Hold a baby and we *feel*: the baby becomes precious, and we bond with it. Embrace the dawn likewise, and what you see becomes precious and sacred. Man cannot hurt that which he holds sacred.

In a way of course, these are just my musings, the personal images that I carry into liminal space. They're not essential to creating a ritual. What matters in ritual is that you *do it*. It's about your presence. Your cosmology and belief system are strictly personal and don't seem to affect the outcome at all. What matters is your truth and authenticity, not any doctrinal qualification or religious status.

That said the images we carry *are* important. Any mystery, when we enter it, works on an imaginal or metaphorical level. Am I speaking to some ancestral presence or some imperilled spirit of place? I don't actually know, but I do know that I hold something in my mind, an image or thought, which feeds and sustains me. And in ritual, once again, it doesn't matter if it is 'real' or not. It is sufficient. My soul, like your psyche, is content with the metaphor and can act upon a symbol.

The image that has been uppermost in my mind, over the last few years, has been that of the elder. Like many of my generation, I've been able to deepen my understanding, and more importantly my experience, of the world. This has left me in the second half of life with a sense of my own worth, but it has also left me, at an important juncture, in a quandary. I'm only too aware that I'm a member of a fortunate generation. The question that has been bothering me is: how do we create elderhood initiations when we have no ritual elders?

~

As is often the way, the question answered itself when a friend of mine, Bob, came up to me at his sixtieth birthday party and asked if I and another friend, Peter, would create him an initiation ritual to see him into elderhood? There was no question. We readily agreed.

In a very real sense, as members of a generation without ritual elders, Peter and I were exploring new territory. The three of us agreed that there would be no timescale – it would take as long as it took. We began to see that there was a ritual to be fashioned out of a review of Bob's life. He seemed fit and confident. We wondered what might be missing.

Bob's Odyssey, which involved over a year of exchanges and calls, meetings and visits to key places, began with explorations of his infancy, boyhood and adolescence. He told his story willingly enough, and made a balsa-wood model glider that smacked of the nineteen-fifties and boys flying planes out on the common, but things deepened when we got to 'First Love'. Bob came up with a *corazón en llamas*, from Mexico, a flaming heart which he wrapped in barbed wire. "I've always found a way to make loving and being loved difficult", he said. It felt like we were getting somewhere.

Next we dived into marriage and career, where Bob got to see the long and worthwhile vista of his life, rather than the disappointments that had previously clouded his view. We were slowly homing in on what was missing, in the hope of providing some sort of *reconciliation* that would enable him to step into elderhood, more comfortable in his skin. Eventually we settled on a wound in Bob's soul, that was undefined but clearly there. As with so many of us, it had to do with his relationship with the feminine.

So, in the still and cold of a Welsh February, we gave Bob the initiatory ritual that he had asked us for fifteen months previously. It was as potent yet tender a ritual as we could devise, centering precisely and delicately on his relationship to the divine feminine. As we worked the ritual it became clear that Bob also needed to say his farewells to his dying mother. He was in an acutely vulnerable place, at one point leaning against the trunk of a tree, head resting against its mossy trunk in quiet communion, as open as a man of sixty could possibly be. The ritual was quiet, dignified and yet powerfully moving. Bob's mother passed away the following day.

When we met later to close out the ritual, we presented Bob with a carved stick that signified his being welcomed, symbolically, to the house of elders. Bob has since moved on in his life, quietly evolving into a different person. He is more relaxed and, even in the midst of later troubles, is more at home in himself. His creativity has blossomed, often an effect of initiatory rituals, and books and poems have flowed from his pen. In his mid-sixties, Bob is living a life that is relevant, rewarding and re-charged. He is an initiated ritual elder.

~

Never before have we been in such need of ritual elders. We need people of all walks of life to develop their skills as holders of ritual, so that they can mature into ritual elders by *doing* the rituals. This means engaging in their own 'ritual development' and working with peers to create the initiations they need to bring them through to elderhood. We may not have had ritual elders ourselves, but we can re-start the age-old processes of initiation that leads to 'elder-making'. The 'Me Generation' are at a point in life where we can give up our supposed selfishness and provide a ritual grounding for our peers, and those who follow. For the most part, we have the money and/or the leisure, to re-enter the world of ritual, spend some time in enjoyable learning, and take up the challenges that only we can address. As Robert L Moore, Professor of Psychoanalysis, Culture and Spirituality at Chicago Theological Seminary writes:

> The human need for ritualization in many areas of life has not diminished. What has diminished is the availability of knowledgeable 'ritual elders' who understand the archetypal human need for ritualization throughout life, and who are prepared to respond competently and effectively by providing ritual leadership to those who need it.[45]

This is not merely an idle notion for ageing baby-boomers. There's an imperative here. Between the unthinking degradation of our environment and our plundering of the planet's finite resources, we are coming to a crossroads where the choice of roads is stark and clear. And that's an entirely different kind of initiation.

~

And what about my own elderhood? I'd been fretting about it since I turned sixty. The notion of elderhood appealed to me, but no male of my bloodline had ever lived beyond the age of sixty. Having lived in the expectation of an early death, I wasn't sure what to do with my life. I grew depressed and restless, which is usually a clue that I need a ritual. Fortunately Annie Spencer, a wise old friend and ceremonialist, reminded me of Jeremy Thres, a friend who leads vision quests on Dartmoor.

I travelled down to Jeremy's place in Devon and we discussed some possibilities. I mooted doing something like an out-sitting, then Jeremy mentioned a 'death lodge ceremony' which resonated deeply. Agreeing to some serious preparation, to see whether I was physically up to it, we evolved a short and powerful two-day death lodge, geared to our culture and my specific needs.

Death lodge ceremonies come down to us through the Cheyenne tradition, though they are believed to have ancient Mesoamerican roots, and are often incorporated into modern wilderness rites of passage, as a segment that involves laying down some out-worn aspect of one's life. As in a vision quest, the idea is to spend time out in the wild, fasting, while waiting for a message. The difference is that you are, symbolically at least, 'dying to the world'.

No sooner had I declared my intention, than death began to gather itself around me. While I contemplated my own death and tried to put my affairs in order, people began dying around me at an alarming rate. By the time I turned up for the ritual I was wide open, grieving and edgy.

Jeremy went through the ground rules. I was to spend a night out on the tops before making my 'descent' into a deep coombe below that would serve as my underworld for the duration of the ritual itself. Jeremy would (unseen by me) check me out if he felt that I might be in trouble but would otherwise hold 'base camp' and await my return. At dusk, Jeremy smudged me and daubed me with white ash to signify my separation from life. At last, after months of groundwork discussion and preparation, I stepped out onto the moor and began dying to the world.

After a disturbed night in which I dreamed of a dead rat, which I picked up and threw away, as far as I could, I awoke to the harsh cawing of a pair of crows. I packed up my kit and headed down into the coombe to seek out the site where I was to settle for the next 24 hours. The crows moved to a distant stand of gigantic silver spruces that were surrounded by blackthorns and a belt of bracken. I followed them. What they led me to took my breath away: a green space, deep in the coombe, walled on either side by moss-covered boulders, overgrown hazels, and great twisted oaks which had ferns and saplings sprouting from the crooks of their branches. As I stood there, in a circle of trees, lost in wonder, I heard the "cronk, cronk, cronk" of a raven, harbinger of mystery. I had found the site of my death lodge. And that's where things started to get weird.

Almost immediately I was assailed by the smell of death. I imagined finding the rat of my dream but the stench came from three large stinkhorn mushrooms behind a fallen log. I thought about moving on but opted to stay put. The floor of the glade was strewn with spruce-cones, and needles. If I lit a fire it would be aromatic enough to mask the smell of the stinkhorns. I set to, preparing the site for my night-long ritual. By degrees I was shifting further and further away from my original intention, which was to simply sit still and pay attention.

I was slipping into an old pattern, of over-work, exhaustion and self-punishment. I had wanted to sit out on the land and listen but, no sooner had I decided that I was going to stay in this beautiful space, than I was scouring the valley for firewood, shifting logs, setting up my camp, lighting a fire and creating a perfect ritual space. For the rest of the day I charged about, moving further away from my centre with every frantic activity. By nightfall I had a perfectly swept ritual precinct, with a sweet-scented fire smoking at its centre, and a huge pile of firewood, and everything imaginable prepared. And that's when it all fell apart, even as the two crows settled above me for the night.

Rather than settle down to pay attention for the night, my ego took me off on a weird and dubious tangent. Somewhere along the line, I'd come up with the harebrained idea that I could summon up my dead. Even as I stood there, I knew in my heart of hearts that I was out of integrity. I had moved from seeking connection to seeking control, from ceremony to magic, and my ego was telling the ritual what to do. In a very real way, I had hijacked my own ritual.

Any medicine teacher will tell you that when you step onto the path of ritual, the spirits will forgive you anything, but put a foot out of line as an experienced ritualist and they'll punish you. It could have been the spirits, though I fancy it was my soul, which knew exactly what my ego was doing, but *something* was lying in wait. I smudged myself with a special South African smudge I'd been given by a friend, and moved to sit on a log facing the fire. As I did so, the log slipped out from under me and I flew backwards with all of my considerable weight. I seemed to hang in space for a second and then my back hit a spruce with a sickening thud. I cried out and crashed to the ground falling spread-eagled onto my collapsed tarp, and my kit. Alone, in the firelight, I discovered that I couldn't move.

As Michael J. Meade, the mythologist, says, "It may have been a long time, or it may have been a short time" but I lay there for a time, watching the fire burn. It was a cloudless night and the temperature was falling fast. Stars twinkled amongst the trees and my teeth were chattering with the cold. I drifted off into an exhausted sleep.

In the Olmec precursor of the death lodge, invented around 1,500 BCE, the last passage of the ceremony was that of the Great Ball Court, in which the individual's soul was passed back and forth, between life and death, by the Lords of Death and Destruction. I experienced no such divine intervention but I still went through what a screenwriter would call a third act climax.

In the middle of the night I awoke to a brilliant light shining into my eyes. I flinched and grunted with pain, only to find that it was the full moon, climbing over the lip of the coombe. As I lay there, listening to the night, I slowly became aware that for all my physical miseries I wasn't afraid: of the darkness, or the wild, or of death for that matter. I felt neither regret nor resentment, just a deep sense of the rightness of things. In that moment I surrendered to whatever came, and was content. I watched the moon heading towards the dawn, and I must have fallen asleep again.

I woke at first light, relieved to find that I could now move. I wasn't paralysed, merely bruised. As I gingerly sat up, I heard a rattling sound coming from the treetops. It was one of the crows. He and his mate were watching me, head to one side, curious, patient, and all of a sudden ugly: these weren't guides or messengers, they were the "Twa Corbies", the corpse-eating crows of the old Scottish ballads[46]. All they wanted were my eyes to feast on. I shuddered, and raised a fist. The crows took flight. As the first of the sun lit the glen I watched them flapping lazily out of my life. I started to laugh.

Up at base camp, Jeremy welcomed me back with hedgerow tea and a quiet concern. Having showered and slept, I sat with him as he de-briefed me; quietly grounding me, exploring the salient points of my story, and checking that I was both well and present. What became apparent was that

I had radically re-thought my relationship with death. As Jeremy said on the way to the station, "It's important to address death, and you've got real about it." I felt I was no longer in thrall to death, nor stuck like a rabbit in its headlights. The paradox was that in reconciling myself to death, I had rediscovered life. On the train home, I looked out at the curvaceous landscape of Devon rushing by and felt a tingle running up my spine. I had never felt so alive.

~

It is morning on Albion Pond. The water is still and covered in a shroud of mist. I am awake and restless so I slip on my crocs and go down to the jetty, taking some sweetgrass that I bought at the Shaker's Fair, some matches, a feather that I found out on Pond Road, and a few pieces of coral blót. September is cooling down the land and across the water I see the first blush of the fall. We will soon be heading back to Britain and another year of work and excitements. I feel sad, and full and very, very grateful. My ritual is simple. I just want to give thanks.

As a kid I found prayers embarrassing. Not that they were intrinsically shameful but, because no one ever taught me how to give thanks, I felt uneasy just asking, and asking, and asking. Today I have a different attitude. The mutual indebtedness of life and the multifarious inter-relatedness of everything makes prayer a natural process, like a robin singing on a branch. The words are scarcely important: it's the tone that matters, the authenticity and the presence.

I light the taper of sweet-grass, face the cottage (which is due north), and work my way through the other cardinal directions, trusting that the words will come – and they come.

> White stone of wisdom in the North,
> Dusted with the frost of care.
> Yellow stone of plenty in the East,
> Bright with the riches of autumn gathering.
> Green stone of growing in the South,
> Alive with the power of what comes forth.
> Red stone of ripeness in the West,
> Rich with the calls of long farewells.
> Four stones made for our remembering,
> Bright stones filled with wonder and awe.

Ancestors, Spirits of Place,
Those who lived here and loved the land:
Spirit of hunter, spirit of settler,
Spirit of wise-woman, spirit of priest;
Spirit of heron, spirit of eagle,
Spirit of moose, and spirit of bear;
Spirit of pine, and spirit of tamarack,
Spirit of maple, and spirit of birch;
Spirit of trout, and spirit of bullhead,
Spirit of rock, and spirit of the reeds.

Thank you, Ancestors, for all you have given us,
Thank you for your gifts, you Spirits of Place.
We are going but we take you with us.
We are leaving now but we will remember.
White stone, yellow stone, green stone, red stone,
Take these gifts as we remember you,
Take these gifts of our work and art.

I take four pieces of blót and gently, respectfully, drop them into the water, as people have been doing on both sides of the Atlantic for millennia. I take a last look at this place that has given me so much. I soak it up, delighting in every tree and plant, and bird and animal, the very rock that I am standing on. I pause and then bow, to close my ritual, then I walk up to the cottage and begin to pack.

"Life's a shedding. Simplicity is best"

References

Chapter Two

1.   As the poet Robert Bly once said, "Just because a man isn't crying, it doesn't mean he's not feeling grief." This is a common thing amongst teenage boys who are often deemed to be unfeeling when in fact they are merely flooded with hormones like testosterone which inhibit the production of tears but not the flow of emotions. See Bly, Robert, *Iron John: A Book About Men*, Addison–Wesley, Boston, 1990.

Chapter Three

2.   The late Catherine Bell quotes Clifford Geertz as approving Milton Singer's observation of Madrasi Brahmins, and non-Brahmins, who, in tune with many medicine teachers, prefer to show rather than tell when it comes to ritual. See: Bell, Catherine, *Ritual Theory, Ritual Practice*, Oxford University Press, Oxford, 1992.

3.   Turner, Victor, *The Ritual Process: Structure and Anti–Structure*, Cornell University Press, 1969.

4.   Roose-Evans, James, *Passages of the Soul: Rediscovering the Importance of Rituals in Everyday Life*, Element Books, Shaftesbury, 1994.

5.   Van Gennep, Arnold, *Rites of Passage*, Chicago University Press. Chicago, 1909.

6.   Brook, Peter, *The Empty Space*, McGibbon & Kee, London, 1968.

7.   For a brilliant and defining anthropological take on liminality, communitas and rites in general, see Turner, Victor, *The Ritual Process: Structure and Anti–Structure.*, Cornell University Press, 1969.

8.   *Star Carr Revisited* by AJ Legge & PA Rowley-Conwy (University College London, 1988) reports on objects that are clearly used for ritual, while *Prehistoric Religion* by Karl J Narr (Britannica Online Encyclopedia, 2008) refers to archaeological evidence from what appear to be very early pre–hunting rituals involving art, sculpture, weapons and a burial.

9.   Blót, meaning to strengthen as well as to sacrifice, is an ancient Norse concept. Though the idea of sacrifice implies the shedding of blood - and while blót and blood have the same etymological root, as does blessing which originally meant to make holy by marking with blood - sacrifice in my evolving practice has more to do with the Central American and First Nation practices of acknowledging by 'giveaway' or mutual indebtedness.

This makes the giving of blót an expression of gratitude, something many of us are short on in our lives.

Chapter Four

10. Al-Anon ACoA (Adult Children of Alcoholics) is a twelve–step fellowship, run on the lines of its parent organisations, AA (Alcoholics Anonymous), and Al–Anon (for the families of alcoholics). Al-Anon ACoA and similar but independent organisations gained popularity during the 90s when it became apparent that growing up in alcoholic families was both traumatic and debilitating. "The Programme" involves a non–religious system of addressing one's hurt and taking charge of one's life through the development of a conscious path through the famous twelve steps, which necessitates: a surrender of the will; a serious look at one's own misdeeds; the taking of personal responsibility; making amends wherever possible, and the evolution of a non-defined 'spiritual practice'. While Twelve Step Fellowships have their shortcomings, it has to be said that, for those without the funds or the inclination to undergo treatment and/or therapy, there is nothing cheaper nor more welcoming than "getting with the programme". For more information visit: http://www.al-anon.org/for-adult-children or http://www.adultchildren.org/

11. Robert Bly's seminal *Iron John: A Book About Men* (Addison–Wesley. Boston. 1990) was a groundbreaker in more ways than one. A critically acclaimed best seller in the US, it managed to reap a minor whirlwind of abuse in the UK where Bly's stand against the Vietnam War and his work with Marion Woodman went largely unnoticed. As a consequence he was often condemned as a right-wing reactionary in Britain, while being perceived as a 'pinko' left-winger in the USA. For naïve, uninitiated men of the Baby-Boomer generation his greatest gift was to move men away from the prevalent victim mentality that was taking hold with the growth of New Age thinking.

12. Lee, John, *The Flying Boy: Healing the Wounded Man*, HCI, Deerfield Beach, 1989.

Chapter Five

13. A Vision Quest, which is not necessarily the same as a rite of passage, is a traditional Native American ritual in which individuals go out into nature, without food, water or shelter for some days, in search of a vision.

See Chapter 13 for a deeper exploration.

14. Macdonnell, A.G., *England Their England*, McMillan, London, 1933.

15. For a beautifully written and compelling plunge into the inner ritual of pilgrimage, exploring the ancient tracks and drove–roads of Britain and beyond, see Macfarlane, Robert, *The Old Ways: A Journey on Foot*, Penguin Books, London, 2012.

16. These words, spoken by the Fisher King as he points the young traveller Parsifal towards the magical Grail Castle, remind us that the magical realm is ever present and nearer than we think, "just down the road and over the bridge". See de Troyes, Chretien, *Arthurian Romances*, Penguin Classics, London, 1991.

17. *A Sussex Poem* from *The Inheritance*, by William Ayot, PS Avalon, Glastonbury, 2013 (pp 19).

Chapter Six

18. See Meade, Michael J., *Men and the Water of Life: Initiation and the Tempering of Men*, Harper, San Francisco, 1994 (pp. 94).

19. Joseph Campbell's discovery and work on a primary mono-myth, which he saw running through all mythologies was a seminal influence on artists as different as Robert Bly (Iron John) and George Lucas (the Star Wars movies). This came to be known as The Hero's Journey. For more on this subject see: Campbell, Joseph, *The Hero with a Thousand Faces*, Pantheon Press, New York, 1949.

20. I am indebted to Steve Banks, a past leader-facilitator of the Everyman/Wild Dance Rites of Passage programme, for permission to quote from his interview with Ron Pyatt: see Banks, Steve, *Achilles Heel: The Radical Men's Magazine*, Totnes, 1999.

21. There is no guarantee of success in a rite of passage. Every now and again a ritual wouldn't gel, sometimes for undisclosed reasons, and sometimes because the participant was unconsciously, or consciously, invested in it not succeeding. If that were the case there would invariably be an enquiry after the event. With the benefit of hindsight, it occurs to me that we did all we could do at the time (and learned some important lessons). The point is that we were dealing with adults who knew that they were not going to be coerced. Things are different in tribal cultures where it is accepted that all will be expected to go through initiation rituals, and that a percentage of participants won't survive.

Chapter Seven

22. My thinking here is based as much on the sacred technologies of Africa as it is on the last century's psychotherapeutic notion of witnessing. For more on this 'spotting' in action around powerful feeling see Chapter Twelve.

Chapter Eight

23. The story of Jumping Mouse is said to be a Native American teaching story, first published in book form by controversial teacher Hyemeyohsts Storm (also Wolf Storm, or Arthur C Storm). Regardless of any controversy surrounding the author, the story has a powerful archetypal 'pull' and is often used in workshops and storytellings. For an entertaining and accessible version of this potent tale, see: Mead, Geoff, *Coming Home to Story: Storytelling Beyond Happy Ever After*, Vala, Bristol, 2011.

Chapter Nine

24. For more on this kind of 'wounded healer' dreaming, see Koss-Chioino, Joan D. & Hefner, Philip, *Spiritual Transformation and Healing: Anthropological, Theological, Neuroscientific, and Clinical Perspectives*, Altamira Press, Lanham MD, 2006.
25. See Campbell, Joseph, with Moyers, Bill, *The Power of Myth*, Anchor Books, New York, 1988.
26. In his seminal book *Ich Und Du*, translated into English as *I And Thou*, Austrian/Israeli philosopher Martin Buber put forward his Philosophy of Dialogue, in which he proposed that we can address the world in two ways; the 'I-It' which implies a transactional *use* of everything, a separation, and a superiority; and the 'I-Thou' that sees everything as in relationship, holistic, mutual, and by extension, sacred. See Buber, Martin (trans Kaufman), *I And Thou*, Charles Scribner & Sons, New York, 1970.
27. I have no evidence for this, but having lived through the souring of the sixties and watched the woozy ceremonials of love and rock turn to violence, drugs and paranoia, I am personally convinced that much of the 'inexplicable' mass violence of the modern world is committed by people in a kind of fugue or trance state, with feelings dulled and minds dissociated by the un-boundaried liminality of modern life and entertainment. For a more formal take on the relationship between

dissociative states and violence, see Moskowitz, Andrew, *Dissociation and Violence: A Review of the Literature* (article), Trauma, Violence & Abuse (review journal), Sage Journals, January 2004.

Chapter Ten

28. At its aromatic best, copal (*tzotzil pom*) is a malleable, resinous incense that is halfway to becoming amber. It comes from the sap of the Bersera tree. It is still held sacred and was used as a powerful incense by the Mayans, the Incas and the Aztecs. There are various types of substance sought and traded as copal in Central America: common or garden yellow copal, known as Mexican Incense, that is used in churches across the region; black copal (*copal negro*) which is heavier, richer in scent; and white copal (*copal blanco*) which has a lighter, sweeter, more citrus smell to it. Golden copal is said to be the most precious of all and was prized by the priests of Meso-America as a means of opening the soul. It is said to promote imagination and creativity and in my experience it is warmer, more evocative than white or black copal. In burning copal it is important to avoid creating too much heat, which causes the melting resin to bubble furiously, giving off a noxious scent like burning plastic or rubber.
29. Round charcoal briquettes are an easily-lit version of the ancient embers our forefathers would have used to burn herbs and resins. They are readily acquired in shops that sell Native American products or ritual paraphernalia. They are usually burned individually in a shell or on a piece of crockery and when lit take a while to 'take'. They also tend to 'sparkle' giving off a chemical, salt–peter smell. Once this burns off, the charcoal quietly smoulders for some time, and is usable once the briquette has frosted over with ash.
30. Shaffer, Peter, *Amadeus* (play), National Theatre, London 1979.
31. Nachmanovitch, Stephen, *Free Play Improvisation in Life and Art*, Tarcher/Putnam, New York, 1993.

Chapter Eleven

32. Potts, Tracy, *Crying the Wrong Tears: Floral Tributes and Aesthetic Judgment*, Nottingham Modern Languages Press, Nottingham, 2007.
33. Muriel Gray, *In Memory of Solipsism*, Article, The Guardian, London, 15 September 2005.
34. Banks, Steve, ibid.

35. For more on these and other developments see McTaggart, Lynne, *The Field*, HarperCollins, London, 2001, or see the full-length documentary film *I Am*, Director Tom Shadyac, Home Made Canvas Productions, Los Angeles, 2010.

Chapter Twelve

36. I am indebted to Jerome Rothenberg for this term. His book *Technicians of the Sacred: A Range of Poetries from Africa, America, Asia, Europe and Oceania*, University of California Press, 1992, was a groundbreaking anthology of earth-based, tribal poetry, which has served me as an important sourcebook for ritual chants and invocations from various cultures. I use the term here because the connection between tribal poetry, chant and ritual is so strong, and the creative energies evoked by both are so very similar.
37. Later, at a debriefing session, it became apparent that many men among us had experienced similar visitations or cross-generational flashbacks from the Great War. The general consensus was that we were shedding the unshed tears of the generations before us who had been cursed with the stiff upper lip, and who were traditionally unable to express their grief.
38. Somé, Malidoma Patrice, *The Healing Wisdom of Africa*, Jeremy P Tarcher/Putnam, New York, 1998.

Chapter Thirteen

39. *The Lacnunga Manuscript*, ref BL Harley 585 MS, British Library, London.
40. Bates, Brian, *The Way of Wyrd*, Hay House UK, 2013.

Chapter Fourteen

41. Homer (Trans E.V. Rieu), *The Iliad*, Penguin Classics Series, Penguin Books, London, 1950.
42. Whyte, David, *The Heart Aroused: Poetry and the Preservation of Soul in Corporate America*, Bantam Doubleday Dell, New York, 1996.
43. Procop, Daniel, *Leaving Neverland: Why Little Boys Shouldn't Run Big Corporations*, Continuum Media, Minneapolis, 2012.
44. In Dante's *Inferno (The Divine Comedy)* Dante is accompanied by the

long dead poet Virgil, who guides him through the descending layers of Hell.

Chapter Fifteen

45. Moore, Robert, *The Archetype of Initiation: Sacred Space, Ritual Process and Personal Transformation*, Xlibris Corp, Bloomington, 2001 (pp140).
46. *The Twa Corbies* (Scottish for the Two Crows) is a ballad based on an earlier English version, *The Three Ravens*, which extols the loyalty of a dead young knight's hawks, hounds and (pregnant) lover. *The Twa Corbies* is a more gruesome take altogether, with neither loyalty nor love, just grief, loss and a juicy snack for the crows.

Bibliography

Abram, David   *The Spell of the Sensuous: Perception and Language in a More than Human World*
Vintage, New York, 1997
Becoming Human: An Earthly Cosmology
Pantheon Books, New York, 2010

Adler, Margot   *Drawing Down the Moon: Witches, Druids, Goddess Worshippers, and Other Pagans in America Today*
Arkana Books, Santa Monica, 1990

Ayot, William   *Small Things that Matter*
The Well at Olivier Mythodrama Press, London, 2003
The Water Cage
Sleeping Mountain Press, London, 1998
The Inheritance
PS Avalon, Glastonbury, 2011
E-Mail from the Soul
PS Avalon, Glastonbury, 2012

Barasch, Marc Ian   *The Compassionate Life: Walking the Path of Kindness*
Berrett-Koehler, San Francisco, 2009

Bates, Brian   *The Way of Wyrd*
Century Books, 1984
The Wisdom of Wyrd
Rider & Co., London, 1996

Beck, Renee
& Metrick, Barbara   *The Art of Ritual*
The Apocryphile Press, Berkeley, 2009

Bell, Catherine   *Ritual Theory, Ritual Practice*
Oxford University Press, Oxford, 1992

Black Elk
(ed J. Epes Brown)   *The Sacred Pipe: Black Elk's Account of the Seven Rites of the Oglala Sioux.*
University of Oklahoma Press, 1953, 1989
(For *Black Elk Speaks* see Neihardt, John G)

Bly, Robert	*Iron John: A Book About Men* Addison-Wesley, Boston, 1990
Bonewits, Isaac	*Neopagan Rites: a Guide to Creating Public Rituals That Work* Llewellyn Pubs, Woodbury Minnesota, 2007
Botton, Alain de	*Religion for Athiests: A Non-believer's Guide to the Uses of Religion* Hamish Hamilton/Penguin, London, 2013
Bradshaw, John	*Healing the Shame that Binds You* Health Communications Inc, Florida, 1988
Brennan, Teresa	*The Transmission of Affect* Cornell University Press, New York, 2004
Buber, Martin (trans Kaufmann)	*I and Thou* Charles Scribner & Sons, New York, 1970
Campbell, Joseph	*Man and Myth* CD. Highbridge Company. *The Hero with a Thousand Faces* Bollingen/Pantheron Press, New York, 1948
(with Moyers, Bill)	*The Power of Myth* Doubleday, New York, 1988
Carr-Gomm, Philip	*Druid Mysteries: Ancient Wisdom for the 21st Century* Rider & Co, London, 2002
Cortesi, David	*Secular Wholeness: A Skeptics Path to a Richer Life* Trafford Publishing, Victoria BC, 2006
Driver, Tom F.	*Liberating Rites: Understanding the Transformative Power of Ritual* Westview Press Inc., Boulder, Co., 1997
Eliade, Mercia	*Rites and Symbols of Initiation* Spring Publications, Putnam, Conn.,1994

Shamanism: Archaic techniques of Ecstacy
Princeton University Press. Princeton, NJ., 1964

Farmer, Steven   *Sacred Ceremony: How to Create Ceremonies for Healing, Transitions, and Celebrations*
Hay House, London, 2004

Foster, Stephen   *The Book of the Vision Quest: Personal*
& Little, Meredith   *Transformation in the Wilderness*
Prentice Hall, New York, 1988

Frankl, Viktor   *Man's Search for Meaning*
Beacon Press, Boston, 2006

Franklin, Anna   *Pagan Ritual: The Path of the Priestess and Priest*
Windrush, 2008

Fulghum, Robert   *From Beginning to End: The Rituals of Our Lives*
Ivy Books, 1996

Goodall, Jane   *In the Shadow of Man*
Dell Books, 1971

Halifax, Joan   *The Fruitful Darkness: Reconnecting with the Body of the Earth*
Harper Collins, New York, 1993

Harrison, Jane Ellen   *Ancient Art and Ritual*
Oxford University Press, London, 1913

Harvey, Graham   *Animism, Respecting the Living World*
C Hurst & Co., London, 2005

Harvey, Graham   *The A to Z of Shamanism*
& Wallis, Robert J.   Scarecrow Press. Lanham, Md., 2007

Hillman, James   *Kinds of Power*
Doubleday, New York, 1995

Hunter, Allan G   *Spiritual Hunger: Integrating Myth and Ritual into Daily Life*
Findhorn Press, Forres, 2012

Hutson, Matthew   *The 7 Laws of Magical Thinking: How Irrational Beliefs Keep Us Happy, Healthy and Sane*
Hudson St. Press, New York, 2012

Imber-Black, Roberts & Whiting (eds)   *Rituals in Families and Family Therapies*
W.W. Norton & Co, New York, 2003

Johnson, Robert A.   *Ecstasy: Understanding the Psychology of Joy*
Harper San Francisco, New York, 1989

Jung, Carl Gustav   *Man & his Symbols*
Doubleday, New York, 1964

Koss Chioino, J D & Hefner P   *Spiritual Transformation and Healing: Anthropological, Theological, Neuroscientific and Clinical Perspectives*
Altamira Press, Lanham MD, 2006

LaChapelle, Dolores   *Ritual is Essential*
Article from *Art and Ceremony in Sustainable Culture, In Context*, Issue No 5. Spring 1984.
Earth Wisdom
The Guild of Tutors Press, Los Angeles, 1978

Lowery, Dave   *In the Dojo: a Guide to the Rituals and Etiquette of the Japanese Martial Arts*
Weatherhill, Boston, 2012

Macfarlane, Robert   *The Old Ways: A journey on Foot*
Penguin, London, 2013

Mahdi, Louise Carus, Nancy Christopher & Michael Meade (eds)   *Crossroads: The Quest of Contemporary Rites of Passage*
Open Court Publishing, Chicago, 1996

McGilchrist, Ian   *The Master and his Emissary: The Divided Brain*
                    and the Search for Meaning
                    Yale University Press, London, 2009

McTaggart, Lynne   *The Field*
                    Element Books, 2001

Meade, Michael J.   *Men and the Water of Life*
                    Harper San Francisco, New York, 1994

Metzner, Ralph   *The Well of Rememberance: Rediscovering the*
                    Earth Wisdom Myths of Northern Europe
                    Shambhala, Boston, 2001

Moore, Robert   *Facing the Dragon: Confronting Personal and*
                    Spiritual Grandiosity
                    Chiron Publications, Asheville. N.C., 2011
                    The Archetype of Initiation: Sacred Space, Ritual
                    Process and Personal Transformation
                    Xlibris Corp., Bloomington, 2001

Moore Thomas   *Care of the Soul: A Guide for Cultivating Depth and*
                    Sacredness in Everyday Life
                    Harper Perennial, New York, 1991
                    A Blue Fire: Selected Writings by James Hillman
                    Harper Perennial, New York, 1991

Nachmanovitch, S.   *Freeplay in Life and Art*
                    Tarcher/Putnam, New York, 1993

Neihardt, John G.   *Black Elk Speaks*
                    William Morrow and Co., New York, 1932

Olivier, Richard   *The Shadow of the Stone Heart*
                    Pan Books, London, 1995

Pearce, Stewart   *The Alchemy of Voice: Transform and Enrich Your*
                    Life Through the Power of Your Voice
                    Hodder, London, 2006

Perry, Grayson	*The Tomb of the Unknown Craftsman* British Museum Press, London, 2011
Plotkin, Bill	*Soulcraft: Crossing into the Mysteries of Nature and Psyche* New World Library, Novato, Ca., 2003
Pressfield, Steven	*The War of Art: Break Through the Blocks and Win Your Inner Creative Battles* Black Irish Books, 2002
Procop, Daniel	*Leaving Neverland: Why Little Boys Shouldn't Run Big Corporations* Continuum Media. Minneapolis. 2012
Restall Orr, Emma	*The Wakeful World: Animism, Mind and the Self in Nature* Moon Books, Winchester, 2012
Roose-Evans, James	*Passages of the Soul: Rediscovering the Importance of Rituals in Everyday Life* Element, Shaftesbury, 1995
Rothenberg, Jerome	*Technicians for the Sacred: A Range of Poetries from Africa, America, Asia, Europe and Oceania* University of California Press, Oakland Ca., 1992
Schrader, Clare	*Ritual Theatre: The Power of Dramatic Ritual in Personal Development Groups and Clinical Practice* Jessica Kingsley, London, 2012
Sogyal Rinpoche	*The Tibetan Book of Living and Dying* HarperSanFrancisco, San Francisco, 1994
Somé, Malidoma P	*Of Water and the Spirit: Ritual Magic and Initiation in the Life of an African Shaman* Arkana, New York, 1995 *Ritual: Power, Healing and Community* Penguin, New York, 1997

	The Healing Wisdom of Africa Tarcher/Puttnam, 1998
Somé, Sobonfu	*The Spirit of Intimacy* Berkeley Hills Books, Berkeley, 1997
Snyder, Gary	*The Practice of the Wild* North Point Press, San Francisco, 1990
Storm, Hyemeyohsts	*Seven Arrows* Random House, New York, 1988
Szacolczai, Arpad	*Liminality and Experience: Structuring Transitory Situations and Transformative Events* Article, *International Political Anthropology*, 2009
Turner, Victor	*The Ritual Process: Structure and Anti Structure* Cornell University Press, Ithaca, 1969
Walker, James R.	*Lakota Belief and Ritual* University of Nebraska Press, Lincoln, 1980
Williams, Mike	*The Shaman's Spirit* Watkins Publishing, London, 2013
Whyte, David	*The Heart Aroused: Poetry and the Preservation of Soul in Corporate America* Bantam Doubleday Dell, New York, 1996
Young, Dudley	*Origins of the Sacred: The Ecstasies of Love and War* St Martin's Press, New York, 1991
Zohar, Danah	*The Quantum Self* Flamingo/Harper Collins, 1991
Zotigh, Dennis W	*Do American Indians Celebrate Thanksgiving?* The Huffington Post Blog. Posted 19th Nov 2012

Acknowledgements

Firstly, I'd like to honour as much as acknowledge my editor Sarah Bird who, in the face of daunting illness and mind-numbing treatments, has risen again and again to the challenges presented by this book. For her grace and equanimity, her precision and determination, I am profoundly grateful. I would also like to acknowledge the following at Vala Co-operative: Peter Reason and Nick Bellorini for honest appraisal and thoughtful support; Rachel Dickens for subtle design work; Denis Kennedy and Alan Blakemore for copy editing; Wayne Sercombe, John Browning and Dawn Jordan for proofreading. Their sharp eyes, faith and time have helped to turn a rough and ragged draft into a book. Thanks also to Ron Pyatt for the cover picture.

I remain deeply indebted to Robert Bly, James Hillman, Michael J Meade and Malidoma Somé for calls and awakenings; to Sobonfu Somé for youthful insights and ancient wisdom; Robert L Moore for sage advice; John Lee for showing a way; Brian Bates for inspiration and the wizardry of connection; Ron Pyatt again, for patience and impeccability; Nicholas Janni for the gift of presence; Lowijs Perquin for attention and context; Richard Olivier for being there, and saying it was time; and Mark Rylance for kindling, and kindness and light in a dark place.

I would like to thank Dr Paul Smith Pickard for a return to sacred landscape; Bernie Gallagher, Ben Judah, Edward Carr, and John Tindall for tribals and other learnings; Fred McGruer, Daniel Dacre and Ivan McFie for quiet triumphs; Jason Wright for seeing something when there was little to see; Steve Banks for the courage to explore; Geoffrey McMullan for true bravery; Mark Dunn for early journeys; Craig Ungerman, Doug Von Koss, and Peter Hutter for a welcome in America; Geoff Mead for sharing the path and walking the beat; Peter Neall for a shrewd eye and the willingness to keep on; Robert Sherman for generosity beyond the call; Eric Maddern, Alex Wildwood, and Justin Kenrick for lighting a fire and passing it on; Simon Roe and Sebastian Kelly for keeping the flame alive; and Phil Atkinson for authenticity, and dreams of Suffolk.

I am grateful to Jim Larkin, Mike Fisher, Mark Goodwin, Michael Boyle, Luli Harvey, John Scaife, Chris Hurn, Victoria Gater, Jane Morrell, and Debbie Collister for help along the way; to Paulette Randall, Stewart Pearce, and Walter Thornhill for insights and open-handedness; Zélie Gross for sage advice; the Reverends Marie-Elsa Bragg and Wendy Carey for care and caritas; Sarah Bolton, Lyle Bolens and Erin Bolens for the creative spirit of family; Tim Malyon for heart and healing places; James Scott-Clarke for benevolences; and Grahame & Sally Davies for wisdom, walks, and breadth of soul.

I would like to acknowledge Parker J Palmer, Philip Carr-Gomm, Prof David Peters, Laurence Hillman, Ben Walden, Nick Ross, Paul Kingsnorth, and Satish Kumar for generosity in thought and deed; Jeremy Thres for hedge-tea and clean ritual; Annie Spencer for quiet wisdom; Tim Shay and family for liberality and insight; Mo Rye for humour and pluck; and Simon Lawrence for trust and constancy. Also Dr Andrew White, Dr Jacquie Drake, and Dr Michael Watkins for the nerve to unleash ritual in strange and demanding places.

Never forgetting the men and women, who have allowed me to create rituals with them during innumerable workshops, initiatory programmes, rites of passage, ritual retreats, breakthrough sessions, and private ceremonies. I am deeply grateful. I am also grateful to those who choose not to be named in this book, to those who can no longer share their wisdom, and to those who never thought of themselves as teachers. Thank you.

Lastly, I would like to acknowledge my wife Juliet Grayson
– for everything.

Lightning Source UK Ltd.
Milton Keynes UK
UKHW041300140121
376964UK00014B/453